DASH Diet Cookbook for Beginners

Low-Sodium Recipes to Nourish Your Body and Delight Your Senses [III EDITION]

Copyright © 2023-2024

Sarah Roslin

TABLE OF CONTENTS

1 INTRODUCTION

DASH, which stands for Dietary Approaches to Stop Hypertension, is more than just a diet—it's a health revolution. Designed primarily to combat high blood pressure, DASH emphasizes a balanced intake of fruits, vegetables, whole grains, lean proteins, and low-fat dairy. By limiting sodium, sugary beverages, and red meats, this plan paves the way for optimal heart health. Benefits of DASH aren't confined to just blood pressure regulation; it also aids in weight management, cholesterol control, and the reduction of diabetes risk. Packed with essential nutrients like potassium, calcium, and magnesium, DASH not only nourishes the body but also fuels the soul. So, if you're looking to not only eat better but feel better, the DASH diet offers a blueprint for a healthier, happier you. Dive in and witness the transformative power of mindful eating!

1.1 DASH to Health: A Food Pyramid Breakdown

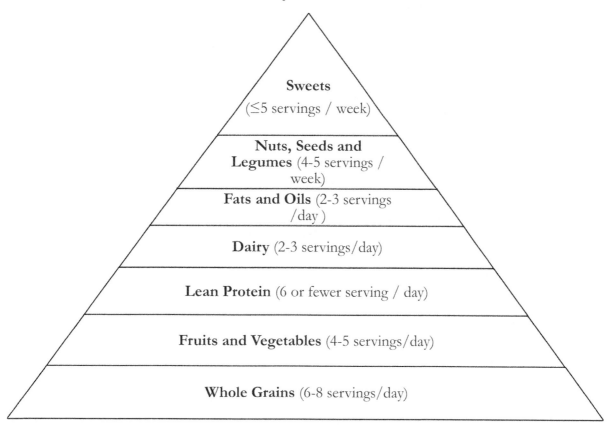

1.2 Stepping into DASH: From Beginner to Pro Guide

Step 1: Understand the Basics

- **What:** DASH stands for Dietary Approaches to Stop Hypertension. It's a diet aimed at reducing high blood pressure and promoting overall heart health.
- **Why:** Beyond managing blood pressure, it aids in weight management, cholesterol control, and risk reduction for diabetes.

Step 2: Prep Your Kitchen

- **Purge the Pantry:** Remove high-sodium, sugary, and processed foods.
- **Stock Smartly:** Prioritize whole grains, fresh fruits and vegetables, lean proteins, and low-fat dairy.

Step 3: Learn to Read Labels
- **Sodium Watch:** Check for sodium content. Ideally, consume 1,500 mg to 2,300 mg daily.
- **Beware of Hidden Sugars:** Syrups, sweeteners, and other forms of sugars can be present even in savory items.

Step 4: Master the Art of Substitution
- **Salt Switch:** Use herbs and spices to flavor dishes. Basil, rosemary, garlic, and oregano can be aromatic alternatives to salt.
- **Dairy Decisions:** Opt for low-fat or non-fat versions when choosing milk, yogurt, or cheese.

Step 5: Cook at Home
- **You're in Control:** Preparing meals at home lets you have complete control over ingredients and portion sizes.
- **Experiment:** Try out DASH-friendly recipes, explore different cuisines, and discover new flavors.

Step 6: Watch Portions and Servings
- **Be Informed:** Understand the recommended serving sizes for different food groups.
- **Listen to Your Body:** Recognize feelings of fullness to prevent overeating. Remember, it's about balance, not deprivation.

Step 7: Stay Hydrated
- **Drink Up:** Water is key. Aim for 8-10 glasses daily.
- **Limit Caffeine and Alcohol:** These can affect blood pressure. Stick to moderate amounts.

Step 8: Be Active
- **Move More:** The DASH diet pairs well with regular physical activity. Aim for at least 150 minutes of moderate exercise a week.

Step 9: Track Your Progress
- **Monitor Blood Pressure:** If possible, regularly check your blood pressure to see the impact of dietary changes.
- **Food Journal:** Keeping a record of what you eat can help identify patterns, strengths, and areas for improvement.

Step 10: Consistency is Key
- **Stay Committed:** Like any lifestyle change, consistency matters. It might take time to see significant results.
- **Seek Support:** Share your journey with friends, join a support group, or follow DASH-centric forums and blogs.

Choice of Foods:
- **Favorites:** Fresh fruits, leafy greens, nuts and seeds, whole grains, fish (especially fatty fish like salmon), poultry, beans, and legumes.
- **Limit:** Red meats, sweets, sugary beverages, and excessive salt.

Avoid:
- Processed foods high in sodium, trans fats, and added sugars.
- Embracing the DASH diet is a journey. Start slow, make informed decisions, and steadily incorporate the principles into your lifestyle. With commitment and knowledge, you'll soon be a DASH pro!

1.3 Dash Diet Vs Other Diets

The DASH (Dietary Approaches to Stop Hypertension) diet is designed primarily to lower blood pressure and improve heart health. However, there are several other popular diets with various goals and guidelines. Here's a comparative analysis of the DASH diet versus some other well-known diets:

DASH Diet vs. Mediterranean Diet:
- **DASH:** Focuses on reducing sodium intake and increasing the consumption of foods rich in potassium, calcium, and magnesium to lower blood pressure.
- **Mediterranean:** Emphasizes heart-healthy fats (like olive oil), whole grains, lean proteins (especially fish), and a moderate intake of wine.
- **Difference:** Both diets prioritize whole foods, lean proteins, and emphasize fruits and vegetables. Both are also linked to improved cardiovascular health.

DASH Diet vs. Keto Diet:
- **DASH:** Carbohydrates, primarily from whole grains and fruits, are an essential component.
- **Keto:** Extremely low in carbohydrates, focusing on high fats to induce ketosis, where the body burns fat for energy instead of carbs.
- **Difference:** Their approach to carbs. While DASH balances carbs, fats, and proteins, Keto significantly restricts carb intake.

DASH Diet vs. Paleo Diet:
- **DASH:** Encourages grains, dairy, and legumes.
- **Paleo:** Excludes grains, dairy, and legumes, focusing instead on foods presumed to be available to Paleolithic humans (meats, fish, nuts, veggies).
- **Difference:** Food inclusion/exclusion based on historical assumptions (Paleo) vs. contemporary health goals (DASH).

DASH Diet vs. Atkins Diet:
- **DASH:** Balanced intake of macronutrients, with no strict carb limitation.
- **Atkins:** Low-carb diet, especially in its initial phase, with a focus on higher protein and fat.
- **Difference:** DASH has a broader, more varied food palette, while Atkins is stricter, especially regarding carb intake.

DASH Diet vs. Vegan Diet:
- **DASH:** Allows for lean meats, dairy, and animal-derived products but emphasizes moderation.
- **Vegan:** Excludes all animal-derived products.
- **Difference:** Animal product inclusion (DASH) vs. complete exclusion (Vegan).

DASH Diet vs. Intermittent Fasting:
- **DASH:** Focuses on what to eat rather than when to eat.
- **Intermittent Fasting:** Emphasizes eating windows and fasting periods. It doesn't prescribe specific foods but rather focuses on the timing of food intake.
- **Difference:** Dietary content (DASH) vs. eating patterns (Intermittent Fasting).

All diets come with their set of guidelines, benefits, and challenges. The best diet is always one that aligns with an individual's health goals, is sustainable in the long run, and is undertaken after thorough research or consultation with healthcare professionals. The DASH diet, owing to its balanced approach, has been widely recognized for its benefits in cardiovascular health and its potential in promoting overall well-being.

1.4 Dashing Through Chronic Health Challenges

The DASH diet, originally designed to lower blood pressure (hence "Dietary Approaches to Stop Hypertension"), has since been found to be effective against various chronic diseases. Here's how the DASH diet interacts with several chronic conditions:

Hypertension (High Blood Pressure):
- **DASH's Role:** The primary aim of DASH is to reduce sodium intake while promoting foods rich in potassium, calcium, and magnesium. This combination helps lower blood pressure in hypertensive individuals.
- **Research Evidence:** Multiple studies have consistently shown the effectiveness of DASH in reducing both systolic and diastolic blood pressure.

Heart Diseases:
- **DASH's Role:** By promoting heart-healthy foods and discouraging saturated fats, trans fats, and excessive sodium, DASH supports cardiovascular health.
- **Research Evidence:** Adopting the DASH diet is associated with a reduced risk of coronary heart disease and stroke.

Weight Management and Obesity:
- **DASH's Role:** Although not designed as a weight loss regimen, the DASH diet's emphasis on whole foods and portion control can aid in weight management.
- **Research Evidence:** Some individuals on the DASH diet report weight loss, particularly when combined with caloric restrictions.

Diabetes:
- **DASH's Role:** DASH focuses on whole grains, fruits, and vegetables, which can help stabilize blood sugar levels. Although it doesn't specifically target diabetes, its principles can benefit those with or at risk of type 2 diabetes.
- **Research Evidence:** Some studies suggest that the DASH diet, especially when paired with sodium reduction, can improve insulin resistance.

Kidney Disease:
- **DASH's Role:** By reducing hypertension, a leading cause of kidney disease, the DASH diet can indirectly support kidney health. However, it's crucial to note that individuals with advanced kidney disease may have dietary restrictions that DASH doesn't address.
- **Research Evidence:** The DASH diet has been shown to reduce the risk of developing kidney disease in hypertensive individuals. However, those with existing kidney disease should consult a nephrologist or renal dietitian before making dietary changes.

Osteoporosis:
- **DASH's Role:** The diet's encouragement of dairy products, which are high in calcium and vitamin D, can help maintain bone health.
- **Research Evidence:** Adequate intake of calcium and vitamin D, as promoted by DASH, is linked to a reduced risk of osteoporosis and fractures.

Certain Cancers:
- **DASH's Role:** The diet's emphasis on fruits, vegetables, and whole grains, while limiting red meats, may provide protective effects against certain cancers.
- **Research Evidence:** High fruit and vegetable intake is consistently associated with a reduced risk of various cancers. While DASH isn't a cancer-specific diet, its principles align with cancer prevention guidelines.

1.5 Food Permitted and Non-Permitted

The DASH diet focuses on nutrient-rich foods and limits those high in sodium and unhealthy fats. Here's a breakdown of foods that are permitted and those that are best limited or avoided, organized by food groups:

Permitted

1. **Grains:** Whole grains: Brown rice, quinoa, whole wheat bread, whole grain pasta, barley, oatmeal.
2. **Vegetables:** Most fresh or frozen vegetables: Leafy greens, broccoli, carrots, Brussels sprouts, bell peppers, etc.
3. **Fruits:** Fresh, frozen, or dried fruits: Apples, berries, citrus fruits, bananas, pears, etc.
4. **Dairy:** Low-fat or non-fat: Milk, yogurt, cheese.
5. **Lean Meat, Poultry, and Fish:** Lean cuts of meat, skinless poultry, and fish, especially fatty fish like salmon, mackerel, and sardines.
6. **Nuts, Seeds, and Legumes:** Almonds, walnuts, flaxseeds, chia seeds, beans, lentils, chickpeas.
7. **Fats and Oils:** Healthy fats: Olive oil, avocado oil, and other vegetable oils.
8. **Sweets:** Natural sweeteners like honey and maple syrup, dark chocolate, fruit sorbets in moderation.
9. **Beverages:** Water, herbal teas, unsweetened beverages.
10. **Sodium:** Herbs, spices, and other natural flavor enhancers, ideally upto 1300mg/day.

Non-Permitted:

1. **Refined grains:** White bread, white rice, pastries, sugary cereals.
2. **Vegetables:** pickled in brine or with added sodium.
3. **Fruits:** Canned fruit in syrup or with added sugars.
4. **Dairy:** Full-fat dairy products.
5. **Lean Meat, Poultry, and Fish:** Fatty cuts of meat, fried poultry, processed meats like bacon, sausages, and salami.
6. **Nuts, Seeds, and Legumes:** Salted or candied nuts, coconut (due to its high saturated fat content).
7. **Fats and Oils:** Trans fats, hydrogenated oils, and excessive saturated fats.
8. **Sweets:** Sweets with added sugars, sugary beverages, candies, pastries.
9. **Beverages:** Sugary drinks, excessive caffeine, and excessive alcohol.
10. **Sodium:** Table salt, high-sodium sauces like soy sauce, salty snacks, canned foods with added sodium.

1.6 Shopping List for Week of Diet

FOOD ITEMS	QUANTITIES
Brown Rice	1 lb.(453g)
Whole wheat bread	1 loaf
Old fashioned oats	1 container
Spinach (bagged)	2 lb. (906g)
Carrots	1 lb. (453g)
Bell peppers (mixed)	4
Tomatoes	5
Cucumbers	3
Cabbage	1
Celery	½ lb. (226g)
Parsley	½ lb. (226g)
Watermelon	1
Pomergranate	3
Banana	7
Pineapple	1
Low-fat milk	1 litre (1000ml)
Low-fat yogurt	1 litre (1000ml)
Feta	½ lb. (226g)
Ricotta	½ lb. (226g)
Chicken breasts	1 lb. (453g)
Canned tuna in water	2 cans
Cod	1 lb. (453g)
Salmon	1lb. (453g)
Shrimps	½ lb. (226g)
Eggs	1 dozen
Lentils	1 lb. (453g)
Black beans (canned)	2 cans
Chia seeds	½ lb. (226g)
Olive oil	1 litre (1000ml)
Mixed herbs (dried)	1
Black pepper	1 pack

2 FAQs

Do I have to eliminate salt completely on the DASH Diet?

No, the goal is to reduce sodium intake, not eliminate it. Focus on using herbs and spices for flavor and be mindful of processed foods, which often contain high sodium levels.

Can I drink alcohol while on the DASH Diet?

Moderation is key. Men should limit to 2 drinks per day and women to 1 drink per day. Opt for red wine for its potential heart benefits.

Is the DASH Diet vegetarian or vegan?

While the DASH Diet incorporates lean meats, it's adaptable to vegetarian or vegan preferences by substituting plant-based proteins.

How does the DASH Diet support weight loss?

While not its primary goal, the emphasis on whole foods and portion control can naturally lead to weight loss when followed consistently.

Are there any foods strictly prohibited on the DASH Diet?

No foods are strictly forbidden, but processed foods, sugary beverages, and excessive salt should be significantly limited.

How soon can I expect health improvements after starting the DASH Diet?

Many individuals notice blood pressure improvements within a few weeks, but individual experiences may vary.

Can I follow the DASH Diet if I have diabetes?

Absolutely! The DASH Diet promotes balanced nutrition that can complement diabetes management, but always consult with a healthcare professional for personalized advice.

Is it expensive to follow the DASH Diet?

The DASH Diet emphasizes whole foods over processed ones. While some items might be pricier, buying seasonal produce and bulk grains can make it budget-friendly.

Do I need any special ingredients or tools for the recipes in this cookbook?

Most ingredients are commonly found in local supermarkets. A well-stocked spice cabinet can enhance flavors without added salt.

Can children follow the DASH Diet?

Yes, the DASH Diet offers a balanced nutritional approach suitable for all ages. However, always ensure that children's specific nutritional needs are met.

How do I track my sodium intake on the DASH Diet?

Reading food labels is essential. Keep a food journal, use apps, or digital tools to monitor daily sodium consumption.

What if I have food allergies or dietary restrictions?

The DASH Diet is versatile. Substitute allergens with alternatives and always consult a dietitian or doctor regarding personal dietary needs.

Will the DASH Diet make me constipated?

No. The high-fiber content ensures you'll be as regular as ever, while the low-sodium diet will reduce problems from excess sodium.

Which fruits and vegetables are best for me?

All fresh produce isgood for you and should be included in your diet. It's best to select the highest-quality foods you can afford.

Can I have any bad foods on the DASH Diet?

No, although it may seem hard at first there are no bad foods as long as they are consumed in the right quantity and proportion to other foodgroups.

Is it possible to drink coffee?

Yes, as long as it is not added sugar or creamer.

What about alcohol?
Alcohol has many health benefits and is fine to have up to one or two drinks a day, butgoing over this amount can be dangerous for your health, so don'tgo over the safe limits that are set for you in phase 2 of the DASH Diet.

How long does it take toget used to the DASH Diet?
As long as you don't add more fat, sugar, or salt to your diet it will be very easy to adapt. Some people take only a few days toget used to the diet, while others take longer.

Can I go on the DASH Diet if I have a history of heart disease?
Yes, as long as you follow all the recommendations of the DASH Diet in terms of healthy fats and low sodium.

What about my sleep patterns?
I don't think it's important to determine how well you sleep every night, as long as you don't try to force yourself toget more than six hours a night, as this may be counter-productive if your body is telling you it needs more sleep than this.

Should I exercise?
Yes, it's very important to exercise on a daily basis for at least thirty minutes if you can.

How will the DASH Diet benefit me physically?
Studies have shown that the DASH Diet cuts down your risk of stroke and heart disease.

How will the DASH Diet benefit me mentally?
A. The DASH Diet will reduce your risk of developing Alzheimer's and other mental disorders by cutting the risk of heart disease.

How will the DASH Diet benefit me financially?
A. The dash diet will save you money as you won't need to buy any processed foods or other unhealthy extras that may come with them.

COLOR IMAGES:
In your DASH culinary journey, accuracy is essential. This cookbook provides detailed recipes and, to enhance your cooking experience, we've also curated a high-definition digital collection of color photographs showcasing each dish. To keep the cookbook affordable, these photos are not included in the print version. Instead, they are available in a convenient PDF format, perfectly optimized for your smartphone or tablet. No need for email sign-up. Simply follow the link provided or scan the QR code below. This allows you to view, zoom in, and download these images for offline use, making your plant-based cooking both easier and more enjoyable. We hope this digital resource enriches your experience and helps you unlock the full potential of plant-based cuisine. Happy Cooking!

LINK: https://BookHip.com/ZNLPAWK

3 BREAKFAST

3.1 Millet Cream

Preparation Time - 10 minutes |
Cooking Time - 30 minutes | Serves - 4

Ingredients:

- Low-fat milk - 14 oz. (414ml)
- Millet - 1 cup (120g)
- Liquid honey - 1 tsp. (5ml)
- Vanilla extract - ½ tsp. (2.5g)

Procedure:

1. Using a medium high source of heat, set a pot in place. Add in the milk and let simmer. Mix in vanilla extract and millet and let cook for about 30 minutes as you stir constantly.
2. Apply a topping of honey to the ready millet cream.

Nutrition per serving:

Calories - 989 | Fat - 2g | Carbs - 38g |
Protein - 6g | Sugar - 200mg | Fiber - 2g |
Potassium - 901mg | Sodium - 189mg |
Cholesterol - 70mg

3.2 The Amazing Feta Hash

Preparation Time - 10 minutes |
Cooking Time - 25 minutes | Serves - 6

Ingredients:

- Hash browns - 16 oz. (448g)
- Low-fat feta, crumbled - 2 oz. (56g)
- Olive oil - 1 tbsp. (15ml)
- Eggs, beaten - 4
- Soy milk - ⅓ cup (80ml)
- Chopped yellow onion - 1 med. Sized

Procedure:

1. Add in 1 tsp. of your oil and scramble egg. Place aside. Saute onions in remaining oil and let cook for 5 minutes.
2. Mix onions with eggs, top with hash browns and serve with crumbled feta, or any other topping of choice.

Nutrition per serving:

Calories - 303 | Fat - 3g | Carbs - 30g |
Protein - 8g | Sugar - 0mg | Fiber - 3g |
Potassium - 525mg | Sodium - 415mg |
Cholesterol - 120mg

3.3 Sausage Casserole

Preparation Time - 10 minutes |
Cooking Time - 35 minutes | Serves - 4
Ingredients:

- Eggs, beaten - 2 med. Sized
- Onion, chopped - 1 med. Sized
- Chili pepper, chopped - 1
- Olive oil - 1 tbsp. (15ml)
- Sausages, sliced - 1 cup (240g)
- Baby potatoes, sliced - 2 cup (480g)
- Chili flakes - 1 tsp. (2g)

Procedure:

1. Mix in sausages, onion, and olive oil.
2. Mix in the remaining ingredients. Let your mixture roast for approximately 5 minutes before transferring to oven.
3. Place in the oven preheated to attain 370°F and allow to bake through for 25 minutes.

Nutrition per serving:

Calories - 74 | Fat - 5g | Carbs - 3g |
Protein - 3g | Sugar - 0mg | Fiber - 1g |
Potassium - 75mg | Sodium - 35mg |
Cholesterol - 84mg

3.4 Apples and Raisins Bowls

Preparation Time - 5 minutes |
Cooking Time - 15 minutes | Serves - 4
Ingredients:

- Blackberries - 1 cup (150g)
- Cardamom,ground - 1 tsp. (2g) (Optional)
- Greek yogurt - 1½ cup (360ml)
- Raisins - ¼ cup (50g)
- Apples, cored and sliced- 2 med. Sized

Procedure:

1. Pour Greek yogurt in the serving bowls, dividing equally.
2. Sprinkle cardamom if using and top with apples, blackberries, raisins and nuts.

Nutrition Per Serving:

Calories - 266 | Fat - 5g | Carbs - 14g |
Protein - 3g | Sugar - 0mg | Fiber - 5g |
Potassium - 374mg | Sodium - 65mg |
Cholesterol - 266mg

3.5 Dill Omelet

Preparation Time - 10 minutes |
Cooking Time - 6 minutes | Serves - 6
Ingredients:

- Low-fat milk - 2 tbsp. (30ml)
- White pepper - ¼ tsp. (3.5g)
- Eggs, beaten - 6
- Dill, chopped - 2 tbsp. (30g)
- Avocado oil - 1 tbsp. (15ml)

Procedure:

1. Using a skillet, heat avocado oil.
2. Using a bowl, mix the other ingredients.
3. Transfer the egg mixture to the hot oil. Allow your omelet to cook for few minutes.

Nutrition Per Serving:

Calories - 71 | Fat - 5g | Carbs - 1g |
Protein - 6g | Sugar - 0mg | Fiber - 0.3g |
Potassium - 109mg | Sodium - 66mg |
Cholesterol - 164mg

3.6 Cheese Hash Browns

Preparation Time - 10 minutes |
Cooking Time - 30 minutes | Serves - 6
Ingredients:

- Olive oil - 1 tsp. (5g)
- Eggs beaten - 3
- Hash browns - 2 cup (480g)
- Vegan mozzarella, shredded - 3 oz. (85g)

Procedure:

1. Whisk eggs in a bowl, mix in shredded cheese.
2. Set a pan on med-high heat, dip the hash browns in whisked egg mixture, and heat until golden brown.
3. Serve with cheese on top with herbs of choice.

Nutrition Per Serving:

Calories - 212 | Fat - 12g | Carbs - 22g |
Protein - 5g | Sugar - 0mg | Fiber - 2g |
Potassium - 328mg | Sodium - 316mg |
Cholesterol - 83mg

3.7 Tomato and Spinach Eggs

Preparation Time - 10 minutes |
Cooking Time - 20 minutes | Serves - 4

Ingredients:

- Low-fat milk - ½ cup (120ml)
- Eggs - 8
- Spinach, freshly chopped - 1 cup (30g)
- Red onion, chopped - 1 med. Sized
- Canola oil - 1 tbsp. (15g)
- Cherry tomatoes, halved - 1 cup (150g)

Procedure:

1. Set a pan in place, add a tsp. of oil and heat, add whisked eggs. Scramble the eggs and add spinach and tomatoes, give a good mix and serve.

Nutrition Per Serving:

Calories - 202 | Fat - 13g | Carbs - 7g |
Protein - 15g | Sugar - 0mg | Fiber - 2g |
Potassium - 354mg | Sodium - 218mg |
Cholesterol - 332mg

3.8 Scallions and Sesame Seeds Omelet

Preparation Time - 5 minutes |
Cooking Time - 10 minutes | Serves - 4

Ingredients:

- Whisked eggs - 4
- Olive oil - 1 tbsp. (15ml)
- Green chilies, chopped - 1 tsp. (5g)
- Scallions, chopped - 2
- Cilantro, chopped - 1 tbsp. (5g)

Procedure:

1. Place a pan over a medium high source of heat. Add in oil and heat. Add in scallions and stir. Sauté for 2 minutes.
2. Mix in the remaining ingredients. Toss and spread the omelet to your pan. Cook until well done on one side for 3 minutes.
3. Flip and continue cooking the other side for a minute, serve with chopped green chilies on top.

Nutrition Per Serving:

Calories - 101 | Fat - 8g | Carbs - 1g |
Protein - 6g | Sugar - 0mg | Fiber - 1g |
Potassium - 97mg | Sodium - 63mg |
Cholesterol - 164mg

3.9 Omelet with Peppers

Preparation Time - 10 minutes |
Cooking Time - 15 minutes | Serves - 4

Ingredients:

- Eggs - 4
- Margarine - 1 tbsp. (15g)
- Bell peppers, chopped - 1 cup (150g)
- Scallions, chopped - 2 oz. (57g)

Procedure:

1. Using a skillet, toss in margarine and heat well until melted.
2. Using a mixing bowl, add scallions, eggs, bell peppers and mix well.
3. Set your egg mixture in your hot skillet and allow the omelet to roast for about 12 minutes.

Nutrition Per Serving:

Calories - 102 | Fat - 7g | Carbs - 4g |
Protein - 6g | Sugar - 0mg | Fiber - 1g |
Potassium - 156mg | Sodium - 98mg |
Cholesterol - 164mg

3.10 Artichoke Eggs

Preparation Time - 5 minutes |
Cooking Time - 20 minutes | Serves - 4

Ingredients:

- Eggs, beaten - 5
- Low-fat feta, chopped - 2 oz. (57g)
- Yellow onion, chopped - 1 med. Sized
- Canola oil - 1 tbsp. (15ml)
- Cilantro, chopped - 1 tbsp. (5g)
- Artichoke hearts, chopped, canned - 1 cup (160g)

Procedure:

1. Using the oil, grease 4 ramekins.
2. Mix all the remaining ingredients and divide the mix between the prepared ramekins.
3. Preheat your oven to 380°F and allow to bake for approximately 20 minutes.

Nutrition Per Serving:

Calories - 176 | Fat - 12g | Carbs - 7.6g |
Protein - 10g | Sugar - 0mg | Fiber - 3g |
Potassium - 238mg | Sodium - 256mg |
Cholesterol - 219mg

3.11 Bean Casserole

Preparation Time - 10 minutes |
Cooking Time - 30 minutes | Serves - 8

Ingredients:

- White onions, chopped - ½ cup (80g)
- Beaten eggs - 5
- Chopped bell pepper - ½ cup (75g)
- Red kidney beans (cooked) - 1 cup (180g)
- Low-fat shredded mozzarella cheese - 1 cup (113g)

Procedure:

1. Using a casserole mold, spread the kidney beans and add in bell pepper and onions.
2. Mix cheese and eggs and transfer to the beans mixture.
3. Allow to bake at a heat of 380°F for about 30 minutes.

Nutrition Per Serving:

Calories - 143 | Fat - 3g | Carbs - 17g |
Protein - 13g | Sugar - 0mg | Fiber - 5g |
Potassium - 376mg | Sodium - 163mg |
Cholesterol - 107mg

3.12 Strawberry Sandwich

Preparation Time - 5 minutes |
Cooking Time - 0 minutes | Serves - 4

Ingredients:

- Low-fat yogurt - 4 tbsp. (60g)
- Strawberries, sliced - 4 med. Sized
- Whole-wheat bread slices - 4

Procedure:

1. Spread the bread with yogurt and then top with sliced strawberries.

Nutrition Per Serving:

Calories - 84 | Fat - 2g | Carbs - 14g |
Protein - 5g | Sugar - 0mg | Fiber - 2g |
Potassium - 124mg | Sodium - 143mg |
Cholesterol - 1mg

4 SALADS

4.1 Shrimp and Veggie Salad

Preparation Time - 10 minutes |
Cooking Time - 0 minutes | Serves - 4

Ingredients:

- Cherry tomatoes, halved - 2 cup (300g)
- Asparagus spears, trimmed - 12 oz. (340g)
- Shrimp, peeled and cooked - 16 oz. (454g)
- Cracker bread - 1
- Watercress - 4 cup (120g)
- Bottled light raspberry - ½ cup (120g)

Procedure:

1. Using a large skillet, add asparagus in some boiled lightly salted water. Allow to cook for approximately 3 minutes while covered. Drain using a colander. Use cold running water to cool.
2. Set the asparagus in 4 dinner plates; add a topping of cherry tomatoes, shrimp and watercress. Drizzle over with raspberry.
3. Add sprinkles of cracked black pepper and enjoy alongside cracker bread.

Nutrition Per Serving:
Calories - 390 | Fat - 14g | Carbs - 38g |
Protein - 29g | Sugar - 8mg | Fiber - 6g |
Potassium - 720mg | Sodium - 620mg |
Cholesterol - 240mg

4.2 Salmon and Spinach Salad

Preparation Time - 10 minutes |
Cooking Time - 0 minutes | Serves - 4

Ingredients:

- Salmon, cooked - 1 cup (230g)
- Lime zest, grated - 1 tbsp. (2g)
- Lime juice - 1 tbsp. (15ml)
- Fat-free yogurt - 3 tbsp. (45g)
- Baby spinach - 1 cup (30g)
- Capers, drained and chopped - 1 tsp. (5g)
- Red onion, chopped - 1
- Pepper - ¼ tsp. (0.6g)

Procedure:

1. Using a bowl, add zest, lime juice and other ingredients, toss thoroughly, place salmon on top and serve.

Nutrition Per Serving:
Calories - 155 | Fat - 1g | Carbs - 15g |
Protein - 22g | Sugar - 3mg | Fiber - 0.5g |
Potassium - 544mg | Sodium - 366mg |
Cholesterol - 200mg

4.3 Corn Salad

Preparation Time - 10 minutes |
Cooking Time - 2 hours | Serves - 6

Ingredients:

- Prosciutto, sliced into strips - 2 oz. (56.7g) (Optional)
- Olive oil - 1 tsp. (5ml)
- Cherry tomatoes, halved - 5
- Red onion, finely chopped - 1 cup (240g)
- Corn - 2 cup (360g)
- Tomato sauce, salt-free - ½ cup (120g)
- Salt - to taste
- Black pepper - to taste
- Garlic, minced - 1 tsp. (5g)
- Spinach, finely chopped - 1 cup (100g)

Procedure:

1. Using a slow cooker, add oil to grease.
2. Add corn, tomato sauce, garlic, prosciutto to the slow cooker as you stir.
3. Set the lid in place and cook for 2 hour on high setting.
4. Add corn to a bowl let cool, toss in all other ingredients, and serve.

Nutrition Per Serving:

Calories - 159 | Fat - 1g | Carbs - 15g |
Protein - 23g | Sugar - 0mg | Fiber - 10g |
Potassium - 501mg | Sodium - 332mg |
Cholesterol - 60mg

4.4 Watercress Salad

Preparation Time - 5 minutes |
Cooking Time - 4 minutes | Serves - 4

Ingredients:

- Asparagus, chopped - 2 cup (340g)
- Shrimp, cooked - 16 oz. (453.6g)
- Watercress, torn - 4 cup (360g)
- Apple cider vinegar - 1 tbsp. (15g)
- Olive oil - ¼ cup (60ml)

Procedure:

1. In the mixing bowl mix up asparagus, shrimps, watercress, and olive oil.

Nutrition Per Serving:

Calories - 264 | Fat - 15g | Carbs - 5g |
Protein - 28g | Sugar - 0mg | Fiber - 1.8g |
Potassium - 393mg | Sodium - 300mg |
Cholesterol - 239mg

4.5 Tuna Salad

Preparation - 15minutes |
Cooking - 0 minutes | Serves - 4

Ingredients:

- Greek yogurt, low-fat - ½ cup (115g)
- Tuna, canned - 8 oz. (227g)
- Cucumber - 1 med. sized
- Parsley, freshly chopped - ½ cup (60g)
- Corn kernels, cooked - 1 cup (160g)
- Black pepper, ground - ½ tsp. (1.5g)

Procedure:

1. Combine kernels, tuna, black pepper, and parsley.
2. Mix in yogurt and ensure you stir properly to get a homogeneous salad.

Nutrition Per Serving:

Calories - 173 | Fat - 6g | Carbs - 14g |
Protein - 18g | Sugar - 0mg | Fiber - 1g |
Potassium - 393mg | Sodium - 57mg |
Cholesterol - 19mg

4.6 Watermelon Salad

Preparation Time - 18 minutes |
Cooking Time - 0 minutes | Serves - 6

Ingredients:

- Sea salt - ¼ tsp. (1.5g)
- Black pepper - ¼ tsp. (0.6g)
- Balsamic vinegar - 1 tbsp. (15g)
- Cantaloupe - 1 med. Sized
- Watermelon - 1 med. Sized
- Mozzarella balls - 2 cup (240g)
- Basil, fresh and torn - ⅓ cup (3g)
- Olive oil - 2 tbsp. (30ml)

Procedure:

1. Scoop out balls of cantaloupe.
2. Add the watermelon, cantaloupe, and mozzarella balls in a bowl, season and serve with mint on top.

Nutrition Per Serving:

Calories - 218| Fat - 13g| Carbs 20g|
Protein - 10g | Sugar - 20g| Fiber - 8g|
Potassium - 430mg |Sodium - 590mg|
Cholesterol - 25 mg

4.7 Orange Celery Salad

Preparation Time - 16 minutes |
Cooking Time - 0 minutes | Serves - 6

Ingredients:

- Lemon juice - 1 tbsp. (15ml)
- Olive brine - 1 tbsp. (15ml)
- Olive oil - 1 tbsp. (15ml)
- Red onion, sliced - ¼ cup (115g)
- Sea salt - ¼ tsp. (1.5g)
- Green olives - ½ cup
- Cucumber, chopped cubes - 1 med. sized
- Oranges, peeled & sliced - 2
- Black pepper - ¼ tsp. (0.6g)
- Celery stalks, sliced diagonally in ½ inch slices - 3

Procedure:

1. Using a shallow bowl, add in oranges, cucumber, onion, olives, and celery.
2. Stir together oil, lemon juice & olive brine, pour this over your salad.
3. Add pepper and salt for seasoning and enjoy

Nutrition Per Serving:

Calories - 65| Fat - 7g| Carbs 4g|
Protein - 0.5g | Sugar - 2mg| Fiber - 5g|
Potassium - 123 mg | Sodium - 43mg|
Cholesterol - 0mg

4.8 Lettuce & Cucumber Salad

Preparation Time - 20 minutes|
Cooking Time - 0 minutes | Serves - 4

Ingredients:

- Chopped romaine lettuce - 2 cup (180g)
- Cooked corn kernels - 1 cup (160g)
- Canola oil - 1 tbsp. (15ml)
- Cooked green beans, chopped roughly - ½ pound (230g)
- Chopped cucumber - 1 cup (160g)

Procedure:

1. Using a salad bowl, add in the above ingredients and mix. Set in serving plates and serve.

Nutrition Per Serving:

Calories - 88 | Fat - 3g | Carbs - 13g |
Protein - 3g | Sugar - 0mg | Fiber - 13g |
Potassium - 302mg | Sodium - 12mg |
Cholesterol - 35mg

4.9 Seafood Arugula Salad

Preparation Time - 15 minutes |
Cooking Time - 0 minutes | Serves - 4

Ingredients:

- Olive oil - 1 tbsp. (15ml)
- Shrimps, cooked - 2 cup (350g)
- Arugula - 1 cup (100g)
- Cilantro, chopped - 1 tbsp. (2g)
- Cherry tomatoes - 3
- Peanuts - 1 tsp (5g)

Procedure:

1. Using a salad bowl, mix in all the above ingredients. Shake well to have a well combined mixture.

Nutrition Per Serving:

Calories - 155 | Fat - 10g | Carbs - 1g |
Protein - 14g | Sugar - 0mg | Fiber - 1g |
Potassium - 84mg | Sodium - 543mg |
Cholesterol - 310mg

5 SOUPS

5.1 Lemon & garlic Soup

Preparation Time - 10 minutes |
Cooking Time - 0 minutes | Serves - 3

Ingredients:

- Chopped and pitted avocado - 1 med. Sized
- Chopped cucumber - 1 med. Sized
- Coconut aminos - ½ cup (120ml)
- Bunches spinach - 2
- Chopped watermelon - 1½ cup (231g)
- Chopped cilantro - 1 bunch
- Lemon juice - 2 med. Sized of lemon
- Lime juice - ½ cup (120ml)

Procedure:

1. In a blender, add in avocado and cucumber and pulse carefully.
2. Add in spinach, cilantro, and watermelon. Blend well.
3. Mix in coconut aminos, lime juice and lemon juice and pulse again.
4. Set in soup bowls and enjoy, with your favorite toppings.

Nutrition Per Serving:

Calories - 101 | Fat - 7g | Carbs - 6g |
Protein - 3g | Sugar - 20mg | Fiber - 19g |
Potassium - 1946mg | Sodium - 228mg |
Cholesterol - 35mg

5.2 Healthy Cucumber Soup

Preparation Time - 14 minutes |
Cooking Time - 0 minutes | Serves - 4

Ingredients:

- Minced garlic - 2 tbsp.(30g)
- Peeled and diced English cucumbers - 4 cup (600g)
- Lemon juice - 1 tbsp. (15ml)
- Vegetable broth - 1½ cup(360ml)
- Sunflower seeds - ½ tsp.(2.5g)
- Red pepper flakes - ¼ tsp.(1.2g)
- Mint leaves - for garnish
- Plain Greek yogurt - ½ cup(120g)

Procedure:

1. Add garlic to a wok in 1 tsp oil, saute, then add lemon juice and spices, stir for 2 minutes.
2. Add the garlic mixture, cucumbers, yogurt and seeds to a blender, blend until smooth.
3. Serve with mint leaves on top.

Nutrition Per Serving:

Calories - 371 | Fat - 36g | Carbs - 8g |
Protein - 4g | Sugar - 6mg | Fiber - 7g |
Potassium - 458mg | Sodium - 240mg |
Cholesterol - 0mg

5.3 Amazing Pumpkin Soup

Preparation Time - 5 minutes |
Cooking Time - 25 minutes | Serves - 4

Ingredients:

- Pumpkin, halved, pitted, peeled & cubed - 1 med. Sized
- Coconut milk - 1 cup (240ml)
- Chicken broth - 2 cup (480ml)
- Pepper & thyme - ¼ tsp. Each (1.2g)
- Roasted seeds - ¼ cup (35g)

Procedure:

1. Using a crock pot, add in all the above ingredients except roasted seeds and set the lid in place.
2. Allow to cook on low for 25 minutes.
3. Set in a blender. Process well to obtain a smooth puree.
4. Add roasted seeds to garnish. Enjoy

Nutrition Per Serving:

Calories - 61 | Fat - 2g | Carbs - 10g |
Protein - 3g | Sugar - 5g | Fiber - 5g |
Potassium - 505mg | Sodium - 254mg |
Cholesterol - 10mg

5.4 Coconut Avocado Soup

Preparation Time - 5 minutes |
Cooking Time - 5-10 minutes | Serves - 4

Ingredients:

- Vegetable stock - 2 cup (480ml)
- Thai green curry paste - 2 tsp (10g)
- Pepper - ¼ tsp. (0.5g)
- Avocado, chopped - 1 med. Sized
- Cilantro, chopped - 1 tbsp. (5g)
- Lime wedges (15g)
- Coconut milk - 1 cup (240ml)
- Coconut flakes - 2 tbsp. (30g)
- Almond, crushed - 1 tbsp. (15g)

Procedure:

1. Add milk, curry paste, avocado, pepper to blender and blend.
2. Set a pan over a medium high source of heat.
3. Place the mixture on your pan and heat, simmering for 5 minutes, or until desired consistency appears.
4. Stir in seasoning, serve with flakes and almonds on top with fresh parsley leaves.

Nutrition Per Serving:

Calories - 250 | Fat - 30g | Carbs - 2g |
Protein - 4g | Sugar - 0g | Fiber - 10g |
Potassium - 487mg | Sodium - 42mg |
Cholesterol - 0mg

5.5 Pumpkin & Garlic Soup

Preparation Time - 10 minutes |
Cooking Time - 6 hours | Serves - 4

Ingredients:

- Pumpkin chunks - 1 pound (454g)
- Onion, dried - 1 med. Sized (150g)
- Vegetable stock - 2 cup (480ml)
- Garlic, crushed - 1 tsp. (5g)
- Coconut cream - 1⅔ cup (400g) + for garnish
- Almond butter - ½ stick (56.7g)
- Ginger, crushed - 1 tsp. (2.81g)
- Pepper - ¼ tsp. (0.62g)
- Parsley, fresh leaves - for garnish

Procedure:

1. In a slow cooker, add all ingredients, leaving some of cream and parsley for garnish. Mix well and cook for 6 hours on high setting.
2. Transfer the mixture to your immersion blender and puree your soup. Serve with cream and parsley leaves on top. Enjoy!

Nutrition Per Serving:

Calories - 234 | Fat - 20g | Carbs - 11g | Protein - 2g | Sugar - 0g | Fiber - 8g | Potassium - 1321mg | Sodium - 326mg | Cholesterol - 0mg

5.6 Vegetable Barley and Zucchini Soup

Preparation Time - 10minutes |
Cooking Time - 0 minutes | Serves - 2

Ingredients:

- Celery stalks, chopped - 3
- Cucumber, cubed - 7 oz. (200g)
- Olive oil - 1 tbsp. (15ml)
- Fresh 30% low fat cream - 2/5 cup (96g)
- Red bell pepper, chopped - 1 med. sized
- Dill, chopped - 1 tbsp. (15g)
- Zucchini, cubed - 10½ oz. (297.18g)
- Sunflower seeds - to taste
- Pepper - to taste

Procedure:

1. Put the vegetables in a juicer and juice well.
2. Add in fresh cream and olive oil. Mix well.
3. Add pepper and sauce for seasoning.
4. Garnish with dill.
5. Enjoy while chilled.

Nutrition Per Serving:

Calories - 325 | Fat - 32g | Carbs - 10g | Protein - 4g | Sugar - 0g | Fiber - 10g | Potassium - 1138mg | Sodium - 477mg | Cholesterol - 56mg

5.7 Vegetable Barley and Turkey Soup

Preparation Time - 10 minutes |
Cooking Time - 23 minutes | Serves - 3
Ingredients:

- Canola oil - 1 tbsp. (15g)
- Carrots, sliced - 5 med. Sized
- Onion, cubed - 1 med.sized
- Quick-cooking barley - ⅔ cup (135g)
- Reduced-sodium chicken broth - 6 cup (1440g)
- Turkey breast, cooked & shredded - 2 cup (280g)
- Baby spinach, fresh - 2 cup (60g)
- Pepper - ½ tsp. (1.1g)

Procedure:

1. Set a pot over a medium high source of heat, add oil and heat.
2. Add in your onion and carrots. Mix well, cooking for 5 minutes and ensure the carrots become delicate.
3. Add in broth and barley and allow to boil. Reduce the heat and let simmer for 15 minutes to make grains delicate.
4. Add in pepper, spinach, and turkey. Combine well and heat for 3 minutes until well done.

Nutrition Per Serving:
Calories - 209 | Fat - 5g | Carbs - 24g |
Protein - 2g | Sugar - 5g | Fiber - 17g |
Potassium - 2397mg | Sodium - 937mg |
Cholesterol - 250mg

5.8 Tomato Green Bean Soup

Preparation - 10 minutes |
Cooking - 35 minutes | Serves - 4
Ingredients:

- Onion, chopped - 1 cup (160g)
- Carrots, chopped - 1 cup (120g)
- Butter - 2 tsp. (10g)
- Reduced-sodium chicken broth - 6 cup (1440ml)
- Green beans, fresh, diced - 1 pound (454g)
- Garlic clove - 1
- Tomatoes, diced - 3 cup (570g)
- Fresh basil, minced - ¼ cup (4g)
- Salt - ½ tsp. (2.5g)
- Pepper - ¼ tsp. (0.6g)

Procedure:

1. Using a vast pot, add in carrots and onion and sauté in a spread for 5 minutes.
2. Blend in the broth, beans, and garlic; heat to the point of boiling.
3. Decrease heat; spread and stew for 20 minutes or until vegetables are delicate.
4. Blend in the tomatoes, basil, salt, and pepper. Spread and stew 5 minutes longer.

Nutrition Per Serving:
Calories - 58 | Fat - 1g | Carbs - 10g |
Protein - 4g | Sugar - 33g | Fiber - 0g |
Potassium - 832mg | Sodium - 203mg |
Cholesterol - 80mg

5.9 Mushroom Barley Soup

Preparation Time - 15minutes |
Cooking Time - 45 minutes | Serves - 4

Ingredients:

- Canola oil - 1 tbsp. (15g)
- Onions - 1½ cup (240g)
- Carrots - ¾ cup (95g)
- Thyme, dried - 1 tsp. (1.7g)
- Black pepper - ⅛ tsp. (0.3g)
- Garlic - ½ tsp. (1.5g)
- Vegetable stock - 8 cup (1893ml)
- Mushrooms, sliced - 1 cup (70g)
- Pearl barley - ¾ cup (180g)
- Dry sherry - 3 oz. (85g)
- Potato - ½ med. Sized
- Green onions, chopped - ¼ cup (25g)

Procedure:

1. Using a stock pot, add in oil and heat. Mix in onions, carrots, pepper, thyme, mushrooms, and garlic. Saute the mixture until onion is translucent for 5 minutes.
2. Mix in veggie stock and barley. Allow the mixture to heat until it boils.
3. Reduce heat and let simmer for approximately 20 minutes until barley becomes tender.
4. Mix in potato and sherry and continue simmering until potato becomes well-cooked for about 15 minutes.
5. Add green onions to garnish.
6. Enjoy.

Nutrition Per Serving:
Calories - 129 | Fat - 5.6g | Carbs - 18g |
Protein - 3g | Sugar - 2g | Fiber - 0g |
Potassium - 562mg | Sodium - 22mg |
Cholesterol - 0mg

6 FISH AND SHELLFISH

6.1 Cilantro Halibut

Preparation time - 10 minutes |
Cooking time - 15 minutes | Serves - 4
Ingredients:
- Shallots, chopped - 2
- Olive oil - 1 tbsp. (15ml)
- Halibut fillets, boneless - 4
- Cilantro, chopped - 1 tbsp. (4.5g)
- Lemon juice - 2 tsp. (10ml)

Procedure:
1. Apply oil to a ceramic pan for greasing. Set your fish inside before topping with cilantro, lemon juice and shallot.
2. Set in oven preheated at 365°F. Bake until done for 15 minutes.

Nutrition Per Serving:
Calories - 365 | Fat - 10g | Carbs - 4g |
Protein - 61g | Sugar - 0g | Fiber - 1g |
Potassium - 1502mg | Sodium - 171mg |
Cholesterol - 93mg

6.2 Shallot and Salmon Mix

Preparation time - 10 minutes |
Cooking time - 15 minutes | Serves - 4
Ingredients:
- Olive oil - 2 tbsp. (30ml)
- Salmon fillets, boneless - 4 med. sized
- Shallot, chopped - 1
- Water - ½ cup (10ml)
- Parsley, chopped - 2 tbsp.

Procedure:
1. Set a pan over a medium high source of heat. Add oil and heat. Mix in shallot and allow to sauté for 4 minutes.
2. Mix in water, parsley and salmon.
3. Set the lid in place and allow to cook for few minutes while heat is set to medium.

Nutrition Per Serving:
Calories - 369 | Fat - 24g | Carbs - 4g |
Protein - 37g | Sugar - 0g | Fiber - 2g |
Potassium - 806mg | Sodium - 97mg |
Cholesterol - 78mg

6.3 Lime and Shrimp Skewers

Preparation Time - 15 minutes |
Cooking Time - 6 minutes | Serves - 4
Ingredients:
- Shrimps, peeled - 1 pound (455g)
- Lime - 1 med. sized
- Lemon juice - 1 tsp. (5ml)
- White pepper - ½ tsp. (0.9g)

Procedure:
1. Cut the lime into wedges. Then sprinkle the shrimps with lemon juice and white pepper.
2. Thread the shrimp and lime wedges in the wooden skewers one-by-one.
3. Preheat the grill to 400°F (200°C).
4. Put the shrimp skewers in grill. Cook each side for 3 minutes until the shrimps become light pink.

Nutrition Per Serving:
Calories - 141 | Fat - 2g | Carbs - 4g |
Protein - 26g | Sugar - 0g | Fiber - 1g |
Potassium - 214mg | Sodium - 277mg |
Cholesterol - 239mg

6.4 Tuna and Pineapple Kabob

Preparation Time - 10 minutes |
Cooking Time - 8 minutes | Serves - 4

Ingredients:

- Tuna fillet - 12 oz. (340g)
- Pineapple, peeled - 8 oz. (230g)
- Olive oil - 1 tsp. (5ml)
- Fennel, ground - ¼ tsp. (0.6g)
- Red onion, cubed - 1 med. Sized
- Tomato, cubed - 1 med. sized
- Bell pepper, cubed - 1 med. Sized (Optional)

Procedure:

1. Cut the tuna and pineapple into medium-sized cubes. Sprinkle the ground fennel and olive oil over the mixture.
2. Thread the tuna, vegetables and pineapple onto skewers and place them on a preheated grill or oven at 400°F (200°C).
3. Cook the kabobs for 4 minutes on each side.

Nutrition Per Serving:

Calories - 135 | Fat - 1g | Carbs - 33g |
Protein - 2.4g | Sugar - 23g| Fiber - 7g|
Potassium - 374mg | Sodium - 151mg|
Cholesterol - 0mg

6.5 Coconut Cod

Preparation Time - 10 minutes |
Cooking Time - 25 minutes | Serves - 4

Ingredients:

- Coconut shreds - 2 tbsp. (12g)
- Cod fillets, boneless - 4 med. sized
- Red onion, chopped - 2 med. Sized
- Red onion, sliced and sauteed - 1 med. sized
- Olive oil - 2 tbsp. (30ml)
- Coconut milk - ¼ cup (60ml)

Procedure:

1. Add the olive oil and let it heat up. Add the chopped red onion and cook for 5 minutes until softened.
2. Add the boneless cod fillets to the pan along with the coconut shreds and coconut milk. Cook for an additional 20 minutes or until the cod is cooked through and flakes easily.
3. Serve with parsley on top, and sauteed onion on side.

Nutrition Per Serving:

Calories - 191 | Fat - 8g | Carbs - 4g |
Protein - 26g | Sugar - 0g | Fiber - 1g |
Potassium - 1502mg | Sodium - 171mg |
Cholesterol - 93mg

6.6 Ginger Sea Bass

Preparation Time - 10 minutes |
Cooking Time - 20 minutes | Serves - 4

Ingredients:

- Grated ginger - 1 tbsp. (6g)
- Olive oil - 2 tbsp. (30ml)
- Sea bass fillets, boneless - 4 med. sized
- Black pepper - pinch

Procedure:

1. Rub the grated ginger onto the sea bass fillets and drizzle them with olive oil.
2. Place the seasoned sea bass fillets on a baking tray. Preheat the oven to 365°F (185°C). Bake the fish for about 20 minutes and serve.

Nutrition Per Serving:

Calories - 191 | Fat - 8g | Carbs - 4g |
Protein - 26g | Sugar - 0g | Fiber - 1g |
Potassium - 502mg | Sodium - 171mg |
Cholesterol - 93mg

6.7 Baked Cod

Preparation Time - 10 min |
Cooking Time - 20 minutes | Serves - 2

Ingredients:

- Cod fillet - 10 oz. (285g)
- Italian seasoning - 1 tsp. (2.3g)
- Margarine - 1 tbsp. (14g)
- Lemon wedges - for garnish
- Parsley - for garnish

Procedure:

1. Preheat the oven to 375°F (190°C). Grease a baking pan with the unsalted margarine.
2. Sprinkle the cod fillet with Italian seasoning, ensuring it is evenly coated.
3. Place the seasoned cod fillet in the prepared baking pan and cover it with aluminum foil.
4. Bake the cod in the preheated oven for 20 minutes or until it is cooked through and flakes easily with a fork.
5. Serve with lemon wedges and parsley on top.

Nutrition Per Serving:

Calories - 150 | Fat - 5g | Carbs - 0g |
Protein - 25g | Sugar - 0g | Fiber - 0g |
Potassium - 400mg | Sodium - 180mg |
Cholesterol - 60mg

6.8 Five-Spices Sole

Preparation Time - 10 minutes|
Cooking Time - 9 minutes | Serves - 3

Ingredients:

- Sole fillets - 3 med. Sized
- Lemon wedges - for serving
- Five-spice seasoning - 1 tbsp. (15g)
- Coconut oil - 1 tbsp. (15ml)

Procedure:

1. Rub the sole fillets with the five-spice seasoning, ensuring they are coated evenly.
2. In a skillet, heat the coconut oil over medium heat for about 2 minutes.
3. Place the seasoned sole fillets in the hot oil and cook each side for approximately 2.5 minutes or until the fish is cooked through and flakes easily with a fork. Serve with lemon and sprinkled spices on top.

Nutrition Per Serving:

Calories - 180 | Fat - 6g | Carbs - 0g |
Protein - 27g | Sugar - 0g | Fiber - 0g |
Potassium - 430mg | Sodium - 159mg |
Cholesterol - 80mg

6.9 Parsley Shrimp

Preparation Time - 10 minutes |
Cooking Time - 10 minutes | Serves - 4

Ingredients:

- Shrimp, peeled and deveined - 1 pound (455g)
- Lemon juice - of 1 lemon
- Olive oil - 1 tbsp. (15ml)
- Chopped parsley - a bunch

Procedure:

1. Heat a pan over medium-high heat, add olive oil, and allow it to heat. Add the shrimp to the pan and cook each side for about 3 minutes until they turn pink and opaque.
2. Mix in the chopped parsley and lemon juice and continue cooking for an additional 4 minutes.

Nutrition Per Serving: Calories - 120 |Fat - 3g
Carbs - 2g | Protein - 22g | Sugar - 0g |
Fiber - 0g | Potassium - 280mg |
Sodium - 140mg | Cholesterol - 190mg

6.10 Tender Salmon with Chives

Preparation Time - 10 minutes |
Cooking Time - 20 minutes | Serves - 4

Ingredients:

- Yellow onion, chopped - 1 med. sized
- Chili powder - 1 tsp.(5g)
- Salt - pinch
- Olive oil - 2 tbsp. (15ml)
- Water - ¼ cup (60ml)
- Salmon fillets, skinless and boneless - 4 med. sized
- Chives, chopped - 2 tbsp. (30g)

Procedure:

1. Heat a pan over medium heat and add olive oil. Sauté the chopped onion for about 3 minutes until it becomes translucent.
2. Place the salmon fillets in the pan and cook each side for about 5 minutes until they are fully cooked.
3. Sprinkle chili powder and chopped chives over the salmon and add water. Continue cooking for an additional 12 minutes.

Nutrition Per Serving:

Calories - 250 | Fat - 10g | Carbs - 2g | Protein - 30g | Sugar - 1g | Fiber - 1g | Potassium - 570mg | Sodium - 75mg | Cholesterol - 60mg

6.11 Fennel and Salmon

Preparation Time - 5 minutes |
Cooking Time - 15 minutes | Serves - 4

Ingredients:

- Salmon fillets, skinless and boneless - 4 med. sized
- Fennel bulb, chopped - 1 med. sized
- Water - ½ cup (120ml)
- Olive oil - 2 tbsp. (30ml)
- Lemon juice - 1 tbsp. (15ml)
- Cilantro, chopped - 1 tbsp. (15g)
- Salt - pinch
- Black pepper - pinch

Procedure:

1. Heat a pan over medium-high heat and add olive oil. Add chopped fennel and cook for about 3 minutes until it starts to soften.
2. Place the salmon fillets in the pan and cook each side for about 4 minutes or until browned.
3. Add water, lemon juice, chopped cilantro, salt, and black pepper to the pan. Cook for an additional 8 minutes or until the salmon is cooked through.

Nutrition Per Serving:

Calories - 250 | Fat - 15g | Carbs - 7g | Protein - 25g | Sugar - 2g | Fiber - 2g | Potassium - 570mg | Sodium - 75mg | Cholesterol - 60mg

6.12 Cod and Asparagus

Preparation Time - 10 minutes |
Cooking Time - 25 minutes

Ingredients:

- Olive oil - 1 tbsp. (15ml)
- Red onion, boneless - 1 med. sized
- Cod fillets, boneless - 1 pound (455g)
- Asparagus, trimmed - 1 bunch
- Black pepper - pinch

Procedure:

1. Preheat the oven to 365°F (185°C).
2. Place the cod fillets in a baking tray and drizzle them with olive oil. Sprinkle the chopped red onion over the cod.
3. Add the trimmed asparagus to the baking tray alongside the cod.
4. Bake the fish and asparagus in the preheated oven for 25 minutes, or until the cod is cooked through and flakes easily with a fork.

Nutrition Per Serving:

Calories - 190 | Fat - 4g | Carbs - 7g |
Protein - 30g | Sugar - 3g | Fiber - 2g |
Potassium - 590mg | Sodium - 90mg |
Cholesterol - 55mg

7 VEGETARIAN PLATES

7.1 Roasted Brussels Sprouts

Preparation Time - 5 minutes |
Cooking Time - 35minutes | Serves - 4

Ingredients:

- Brussels sprouts, halved trimmed - 1½ pounds (680g)
- Olive oil - 2 tbsp. (30ml)
- Salt - ¼ tsp. (1.25g)
- Black pepper, freshly ground - ½ tsp. (1.25g)

Procedure:

1. Preheat your oven to 400°F. Using a mixing bowl, mix in Brussels sprouts and olive oil. Toss well to evenly coat.
2. Set Brussels sprouts to a large baking sheet. Flip them over, so the cut-side faces down with the flat part touching the baking sheet. Sprinkle pepper and salt to the mixture.
3. Bake within 30 minutes to ensure the Brussels sprouts become crispy and lightly charred to the outside while toasted to the bottom side. Serve.

Nutrition Per Serving:

Calories - 134 | Fat - 8g | Carbs - 15g |
Protein - 6g | Sugar - 0g | Fiber - 27g |
Potassium - 662mg | Sodium - 189mg |
Cholesterol - 0mg

7.2 Chunky Black-Bean Dip

Preparation Time - 5 minutes |
Cooking Time - 1 minutes | Serves - 2

Ingredients:

- Black beans, drained, with liquid reserved - 15 oz. (425g)
- Chipotle peppers in adobo sauce - ½ can
- Plain Greek yogurt - ¼ cup (60g)
- Black pepper, ground - ¼ tsp. (0.5g)

Procedure:

1. Using a blender, add in chipotle peppers, yogurt and beans. Mix well before processing to obtain a smooth consistency. Mix in part of reserved bean liquid (a tablespoon at a moment) to obtain a thinner consistency.
2. Add black pepper for seasoning and enjoy.

Nutrition Per Serving:

Calories - 70 | Fat - 1g | Carbs - 11g |
Protein - 5g | Sugar - 5g | Fiber - 24g |
Potassium - 281mg | Sodium - 159mg |
Cholesterol - 12mg

7.3 Greek Flat bread with Spinach, Tomatoes & Feta

Preparation Time - 15 minutes |
Cooking Time - 9 minutes | Serves - 2

Ingredients:

- Baby spinach, fresh and coarsely chopped - 2 cup (60g)
- Olive oil - 2 tsp. (10ml)
- Naan or flat bread - 2 slices
- Black olives, sliced - ¼ cup (37.5g)
- Plum tomatoes, sliced - 2 med. sized
- Italian seasoning blend (salt-free) - ½ tsp. (1g)
- Feta, crumbled - ¼ cup (37.5g)

Procedure:

1. Preheat oven to attain 400°F. Using a skillet set in place over the medium high heat, add in 3 tbsp.. water and heat. Mix in spinach, and steam for 2 minutes to wilt while covered. Drain any water in excess before placing aside.
2. Drizzle flat breads with oil. To each of the flat bread, add olives, seasoning, spinach, feta and tomatoes to top. Bake until browned for 7 minutes. Slice in 4 pieces and enjoy.

Nutrition Per Serving:

Calories - 410 | Fat - 16g | Carbs - 53g |
Protein - 16g | Sugar - 2g | Fiber - 7g |
Potassium - 521mg | Sodium - 622mg |
Cholesterol - 28mg

7.4 Black-Bean and Vegetable Burrito

Preparation Time - 15 minutes |
Cooking Time - 15 minutes | Serves - 4

Ingredients:

- olive oil - ½ tbsp. (7.5ml)
- chopped red or green bell peppers - 2 med. sized
- diced zucchini or summer squash - 1 med. sized
- chili powder - ½ tsp. (1g)
- cumin - 1 tsp. (2g)
- ground black pepper - ¼ tsp. (0.5g)
- drained and rinsed black beans - 2 (14 oz.) cans (28oz.) (795g)
- halved cherry tomatoes - 1 cup (150g)
- whole-wheat tortillas - 4-8 inch
- Optional for Serving - spinach, chopped scallions, sliced avocado, or hot sauce

Procedure:

1. Set a saute pan on a medium high source of heat. Add in oil and heat. Mix in bell peppers and saute for 4 minutes until crisp and tender. Add the zucchini, chili powder, cumin, and black pepper, and continue to sauté for 5 minutes until vegetables become tender.
2. Add the black beans and cherry tomatoes and cook within 5 minutes. Divide between 4 burritos and serve topped with optional ingredients as desired. Enjoy immediately.

Nutrition Per Serving:

Calories - 311 | Fat - 6g | Carbs - 52g |
Protein - 19g | Sugar - 0g | Fiber - 22g |
Potassium - 329mg | Sodium - 199mg |
Cholesterol - 0mg

7.5 Red Beans and Rice

Preparation Time - 5 minutes |
Cooking Time - 30 minutes | Serves - 2

Ingredients:

- Brown rice - ½ cup (95g)
- Water, - 1 cup plus extra ¼ cup (240+60ml)
- Red beans, drained - 1 (14 oz.) can (400g)
- Cumin, ground - 1 tbsp. (8g)
- Lime juice - of 1 lime
- Fresh spinach - 4 handfuls
- Optional toppings - Greek yogurt, avocado, chopped tomatoes, onions

Procedure:

1. Using a pot, mix rice plus water and let boil. Cover and lower your heat to a low simmer. Cook within 20 to 25 minutes or as per the directions on the package.
2. Meanwhile, add the beans, ¼ cup water, lime juice, and cumin to a medium skillet. Simmer within 5 to 7 minutes.
3. Once the liquid is reduced considerably, remove from the heat. Mix in spinach and allow to wilt for 3 minutes while covered. Add in beans and mix well. Enjoy alongside rice with toppings of your choice.

Nutrition Per Serving:

Calories - 232 | Fat - 2g | Carbs - 41g |
Protein - 13g | Sugar - 0g | Fiber - 21.71g |
Potassium - 367mg | Sodium - 210mg |
Cholesterol - 0mg

7.6 Veggie Pita Rolls

Preparation Time - 30 minutes|
Cooking Time - 0 minutes | Serves - 2

Ingredients:

- Romaine lettuce, shredded - 1 cup (30g)
- Cucumber, chopped - ½ cup (50g)
- Red onion, chopped - 1 med. sized
- Olive oil - 1 tbsp. (15ml)
- Black pepper - ¼ tsp. (0.5g)
- Prepared hummus - ¼ cup (60g)
- Bell pepper, chopped and pitted - 1 med. sized
- Tomato, chopped - 1 med. sized
- Garlic clove, finely minced - 1
- Fresh lime juice - ½ tbsp. (7.5ml)
- Whole-wheat pita breads, warmed - 2

Procedure:

1. Using a bowl, mix in the above ingredients with exception of pitas and hummus. Toss gently and ensure they are well coated. Place each pita bread onto serving plates.
2. Spread 2 tbsp. of hummus over a pita bread evenly. Top with salad and roll the pita bread.
3. Repeat with remaining pita bread, hummus and salad.

Nutrition Per Serving:

Calories - 334 | Fat - 12g | Carbs - 52g |
Protein - 11g | Sugar - 7g | Fiber - 9g |
Potassium - 587mg | Sodium - 400mg |
Cholesterol - 0mg

7.7 Veggies Stuffed Bell Peppers

Preparation Time - 15 minutes |
Cooking Time - 25 minutes | Serves – 4

Ingredients:

- Fresh shiitake mushrooms - ½ lb. (230g)
- Garlic cloves - 2
- Olive oil - 2 tbsp. (30ml)
- Black pepper - ¼ tsp. (0.5g)
- Celery stalk - 1 cup (120g)
- Unsalted walnuts - ½ cup (50g)
- Salt - pinch
- Bell peppers, halved and pitted - 4 med. sized

Procedure:

1. Preheat oven to attain 400 °F grease your baking sheet.
2. Using a food processor, mix in oil, salt, mushrooms, celery, garlic, walnuts, pepper and pulse to finely chop. Stuff bell peppers with the mushroom mixture.
3. Set them onto the prepared baking sheet. Bake until slightly brown for about 25 minutes. Enjoy while warm.

Nutrition Per Serving:

Calories - 213 | Fat - 17g | Carbs - 14g |
Protein - 7g | Sugar - 7g | Fiber - 4g |
Potassium - 456mg | Sodium - 160mg |
Cholesterol - 0mg

7.8 Rosemary Endives

Preparation Time - 10 minutes |
Cooking Time - 20 Minutes | Serves - 4

Ingredients:

- Olive oil - 2 tbsp. (30ml)
- Dried rosemary - 1 tsp. (1.7g)
- Endives, halved - 2
- Black pepper - ¼ tsp. (0.5g)
- Turmeric powder - ½ tsp. (1.4g)

Procedure:

1. Using a baking pan, mix all ingredients as you toss for maximum coating. Set in your preheated oven to attain 400 °F and let bake well for 20 minutes.
2. Enjoy.

Nutrition Per Serving:

Calories - 66 | Fat - 7g | Carbs - 1g |
Protein - 0.3g | Sugar - 1.3g | Fiber - 2g |
Potassium - 411mg | Sodium - 113mg |
Cholesterol - 0mg

7.9 Easy Chickpea Veggie Burgers

Preparation Time - 10 minutes | Cooking Time - 20 minutes | Serves - 4

Ingredients:

- Chickpeas, drained and rinsed - 1 (15 oz) can (425g)
- Onion powder - 1 tsp. (2.3g)
- Frozen spinach, thawed - ½ cup (95g)
- Rolled oats - ⅓ cup (26.4g)
- Garlic powder - 1 tsp. (2.8g)

Procedure:

1. Set your oven to preheat to attain 400°F. Set a parchment paper to your baking sheet.
2. Using a mixing bowl, add half of the beans and mash until fairly smooth.
3. In a blender, add the remaining beans, spinach, oats, and spices. Blend until pureed. Add mixture to the bowl of mashed beans and stir until well combined.
4. Divide in 4 equal sections and form patties. Bake for 7 to 10 minutes. Carefully flip and bake until crusty on the outside for extra 10 minutes.
5. Place on a wholegrain bun with your favorite toppings.

Nutrition Per Serving:

Calories - 118 | Fat - 1g | Carbs - 10g | Protein - 7g | Sugar - 0g | Fiber - 17g | Potassium - 583mg | Sodium - 108mg | Cholesterol - 7mg

7.10 Baked Sweet Potatoes with Cumin

Preparation Time - 15 minutes | Cooking Time - 20 minutes | Serves - 4

Ingredients:

- Sweet potatoes - 4 med. sized
- Freshly ground black pepper - ¼ tsp. (0.5g)
- Red onion, diced - ½ med. sized
- Low-fat or nonfat plain Greek yogurt - ½ cup (120g)
- Olive oil - 1 tsp. (5ml)
- Red bell pepper, diced - 1 med. sized
- Ground cumin - 1 tsp. (2g)
- Chickpeas, drained and rinsed - 1 (15 oz.) can (425g)

Procedure:

1. Prick the potatoes using a fork and cook on potato setting of the microwave for 10 minutes until well cooked and potatoes become soft.
2. Using a bowl, add in black pepper and yogurt and combine. Set a pot over a medium source of heat, add in oil and heat. Add in cumin, bell pepper, onion and an extra black pepper to enhance the taste.
3. Add in the chickpeas, stir well to combine, and allow the mixture to cook for 5 minutes. Slice potatoes midway lengthwise down and top each half with a portion of the bean mixture followed by 1 to 2 tbsp.. of the yogurt. Serve immediately.

Nutrition Per Serving:

Calories - 264 | Fat - 2g | Carbs - 51g | Protein - 12g | Sugar - 16g | Fiber - 23g | Potassium - 78mg | Sodium - 124mg | Cholesterol - 3mg

7.11 White Beans with Spinach and Pan-Roasted Tomatoes

Preparation Time - 15 minutes |
Cooking Time - 11 minutes | Serves - 2

Ingredients:

- Olive oil - 1 tbsp. (15ml)
- Plum tomatoes, halved - 4
- Frozen spinach, defrosted and squeezed of excess water - 10 oz. (285g)
- Garlic cloves, thinly sliced - 2
- Water - 2 tbsp. (30ml)
- Black pepper, freshly ground - ¼ tsp. (0.6g)
- White beans, drained - 1 can (230g)
- Lemon juice - of 1 lemon

Procedure:

1. Add and heat oil in your nonstick skillet set over a medium high source of heat. Add tomatoes, the cut-side should face down, and let cook within 5 minutes. You then flip to the second side and cook within 1 more minute. Set on a plate.
2. Lower your heat towards medium setting and mix in spinach, pepper, water, and garlic. Cook as you toss for 3 minutes to ensure the spinach is cooked through.
3. Take back the tomatoes to your skillet, add the white beans and lemon juice, toss well until heated for 2 minutes.

Nutrition Per Serving:

Calories - 293 | Fat - 9g | Carbs - 43g |
Protein - 15g | Sugar - 0g | Fiber - 16g |
Potassium - 78mg | Sodium - 267mg |
Cholesterol - 0mg

7.12 Black-Eyed Peas and Greens Power Salad

Preparation Time - 15 minutes |
Cooking Time - 6 minutes | Serves - 2

Ingredients:

- Olive oil - 1 tbsp. (15ml)
- Juice of ½ lemon
- Purple cabbage, chopped - 3 cup (360g)
- Baby spinach - 5 cup (150g)
- Salt - ¼ tsp. (1.5g)
- Carrots, shredded - 1 cup (110g)
- Black-eyed peas, drained - 1 can (240g)
- Ground black pepper - ¼ tsp. (0.6g)

Procedure:

1. In a medium pan, add oil and cabbage and sauté for 2 minutes while on the medium heat setting. Add in your spinach, cook for 4 minutes while covered until the greens become wilted. Once done, transfer to a bowl.
2. Mix in peas, carrots, juice, pepper and salt as you toss well.

Nutrition Per Serving:

Calories - 320 | Fat - 9g | Carbs - 49g |
Protein - 16g | Sugar - 1g | Fiber - 23g |
Potassium - 544mg | Sodium - 351mg |
Cholesterol - 10mg

7.13 Butternut-Squash Macaroni and Cheese

Preparation Time - 15 min |
Cooking Time - 20 minutes | Serves - 2
Ingredients:

- Ziti macaroni, whole-wheat - 1 cup (200g)
- Olive oil - 1 tbsp. (15ml)
- Butternut squash, cubed - 2 cup (360g)
- Non-fat milk - 1 cup (240g)
- Black pepper - ¼ tsp. (0.6g)
- Dijon mustard - 1 tsp. (5g)
- Low-fat cheddar cheese, shredded - ¼ cup (28g)

Procedure:
1. Cook your pasta al dente using a pot with boiling water. Drain pasta and place aside. Using a saucepan set on a medium high source of heat, mix ½ cup milk and butternut squash. Add black pepper for seasoning. Allow to simmer. Reduce heat intensity and continue cooking for 10 minutes.
2. Using a blender, mix in Dijon mustard and squash. Purée well to obtain a smooth consistency. Meanwhile, using a sauté pan set on medium heat, mix in olive oil, the squash purée and the rest of the milk. Simmer for 5 minutes before stirring in the cheese.
3. Add in your pasta as you stir. Enjoy right away.

Nutrition Per Serving:
Calories - 373 | Fat - 10g | Carbs - 59g | Protein - 14g | Sugar - 21g | Fiber - 12g | Potassium - 56mg | Sodium - 330mg | Cholesterol - 7mg

7.14 Pasta with Peas & Tomatoes

Preparation Time - 15 minutes |
Cooking Time - 15 minutes | Serves - 2
Ingredients:

- Whole-grain pasta of choice - ½ cup (60g)
- Water - 8 cup (1920ml) plus ¼ cup (60ml) for finishing
- Frozen peas - 1 cup (160g)
- Olive oil - 1 tbsp. (15ml)
- Cherry tomatoes, halved - 1 cup (150g)
- Ground black pepper - ¼ tsp. (0.6g)
- Dried basil - 1 tsp. (1g)
- Parmesan cheese (low-sodium), grated - ¼ cup (28g)

Procedure:
1. Cook your pasta accordingly until al dente. Add the water to the same pot you used to cook the pasta, and when it's boiling, add the peas. Cook within 5 minutes before draining and setting aside until ready.
2. Using a nonstick skillet set over medium source of heat. Pour in oil and heat. Mix in cherry tomatoes, set lid in place and allow the tomatoes to soften for 5 minutes as you occasionally stir.
3. Add in basil and black pepper for seasoning. Toss in peas, pasta, and ¼ cup of water, stir and remove from heat. Enjoy with a topping of Parmesan.

Nutrition Per Serving:
Calories - 266 | Fat - 12g | Carbs - 30g | Protein - 13g | Sugar - 12g | Fiber - 11g | Potassium - 67mg | Sodium - 320mg | Cholesterol - 5mg

7.15 Healthy Vegetable Fried Rice

Preparation Time - 15 minutes |
Cooking Time - 10 minutes | Serves - 4
Ingredients:
For sauce -

- Garlic vinegar - ⅓ cup (80ml)
- Dark molasses - 1½ tbsp. (30g)
- Onion powder - 1 tsp. (2.3g)

For the fried rice -

- Olive oil - 1 tsp. (5ml)
- Whole eggs, lightly beaten - 2 + 4 egg whites
- Frozen mixed vegetables - 1 cup (160g)
- Frozen edamame - 1 cup (160g)
- Cooked brown rice - 2 cup (380g)

Procedure:

1. To prepare sauce, mix the garlic vinegar, molasses, and onion powder in a glass jar. Shake well.
2. Using a skillet set over a medium high source of heat, add in oil and heat. Set in eggs and egg whites, cook for 1 minute until the eggs set.
3. Use a spoon to break eggs into small pieces. Mix in edamame and mixed vegetables. Cook as you stir for approximately 4 minutes.
4. Mix in the sauce and brown rice to your veggie-egg mixture and cook until well done for 5 minutes. Serve immediately.

Nutrition Per Serving:
Calories - 210 | Fat - 6g | Carbs - 28g |
Protein - 13g | Sugar - 15g | Fiber - 18g |
Potassium - 78mg | Sodium - 113mg |
Cholesterol - 372mg

7.16 Cast Iron Roots and Grain

Preparation Time - 10 minutes |
Cooking Time - 30 minutes | Serves - 4
Ingredients:

- Olive oil - 2 tbsp. (30ml)
- Honey - 2 tsp. (10g)
- Rainbow carrots, sliced - 2 cup (260g)
- Beets, sliced - 1 cup (150g)
- Turnips, chopped - 1 cup (130g)
- Onion, sliced - 1 cup (160)
- Fresh tarragon - 1 tbsp. (2g)
- Dried lavender - 1 tsp. (1.6g)
- Low sodium vegetable broth - 4 cup (960ml)
- Bulgur - 1½ cup (270g)

Procedure:

1. Set a cast iron skillet over a medium high source of heat and heat well.
2. Using a bowl, combine the beets, turnips, carrots, and onion. Drizzle over the honey and olive oil. Add tarragon and lavender for seasoning. Toss well to ensure well coated.
3. Add the vegetables to your skillet and cook until slightly tender, approximately 10 minutes.
4. Mix in vegetable broth and allow to boil.
5. Mix in the bulgur and reduce your heat to low. Simmer for 15 minutes while covered until bulgur becomes tender.

Nutrition Per Serving:
Calories - 312 | Fat - 9g | Carbs - 56g |
Protein - 7.9g | Sugar - 11g | Fiber - 14g |
Potassium - 594mg | Sodium - 241mg |
Cholesterol - 0mg

7.17 Easy Beet and Goat Cheese Risotto

Preparation Time - 10 minutes |
Cooking Time - 30 minutes | Serves - 4
Ingredients:

- Olive oil - ¼ cup (60ml)
- Beets, diced - 1½ cup (225g)
- Red onion, diced - 1 cup (160g)
- Spinach, chopped - 2 cup (60g)
- Arborio rice - 1 cup (200g)
- Low sodium vegetable broth - 2 cup (480ml)
- Fresh rosemary, chopped - 2 tsp. (1.6g)
- Goat cheese - ½ cup (112g)
- Walnuts, chopped - ¼ cup (30g)

Procedure:

1. Using a saucepan set over a medium source of heat, add olive oil and heat.
2. Add in onions and beets. Sauté until tender, approximately 5 minutes.
3. Mix in spinach and cook for 3 more minutes.
4. Add in rice and continue cooking as you stir for 3 minutes, to lightly toast the rice.
5. Next, add the vegetable broth and rosemary. Increase the heat to ensure the broth boils.
6. Reduce your heat intensity to low, and continue cooking as you stir occasionally, until the rice has a soft but firm texture.
7. Take out from the heat and stir in goat cheese.
8. Garnish with chopped walnuts for serving.

Nutrition Per Serving:

Calories - 412.5 | Fat - 35.2g | Carbs - 27g | Protein - 11g | Sugar - 16.9g | Fiber - 5g | Potassium - 353mg | Sodium - 257mg | Cholesterol - 78mg

7.18 Mushroom and Eggplant Casserole

Preparation Time - 10 minutes |
Cooking Time - 30 minutes | Serves - 4
Ingredients:

- Eggplant, sliced - 1 pound (454g)
- Olive oil - 1 tbsp. (15ml)
- Yellow onion, chopped - 1 cup (160g)
- Garlic cloves, crushed and minced - 3
- Oregano, dried - 1 tsp. (1g)
- Black pepper - ½ tsp. (1.2g)
- Mushrooms, sliced - 3 cup (435g)
- Tomato sauce (low sodium) - 1 cup (240g)
- Cooked cauliflower rice - 2 cup (380g)
- Low fat mozzarella cheese - 1 cup (112g)
- Asiago cheese, grated - ½ cup (56g)
- Fresh chopped basil - ¼ cup (10g)

Procedure:

1. Preheat your oven to 375°F (190°C).
2. In a nonstick skillet over medium-high heat, heat olive oil.
3. Add eggplant slices and cook each side for 3 minutes. Set aside.
4. In the same skillet, add garlic, oregano, onion, and black pepper. Sauté for 4 minutes until onions are tender. Add mushrooms and cook an additional 3 minutes.
5. Lightly oil an 8x8 baking dish and spread a thin layer of tomato sauce on the bottom.
6. Create layers in the baking dish with eggplant slices, cauliflower rice, mozzarella cheese, and mushrooms, repeating until all ingredients are used.
7. For the final layer, top with mozzarella cheese, Asiago cheese, and fresh basil.
8. Place the casserole in the oven and bake for 20 minutes.

Nutrition Per Serving:

Calories - 340 | Fat - 14g | Carbs - 15g | Protein - 23g | Sugar - 5g | Fiber - 7g | Potassium - 404mg | Sodium - 194mg | Cholesterol - 62mg

7.19 Spinach Soufflés

Preparation time - 15 minutes |
Cooking time - 1 h & 20 min | Serves - 4
Ingredients

- egg whites - 4
- dried parsley - 1 tsp.(1.2g)
- cream of tartar - ¼ tsp. (1g)
- Almond flour - 1 tbsp.(15g) + 1½ tsp. (7.5g)
- Garlic, minced - 1 tsp. (4g)
- Parmesan cheese - 2 oz. (56g)
- Baby spinach - 6 oz. (170g)
- Coconut flour - 2 tbsp. (16g)
- Black pepper - ⅛ tsp. (0.8g)
- Egg yolks - 2

Procedure:

1. Preheat your oven to 425°F (220°C).
2. Grease 4 ramekins (6 oz. each) with oil and sprinkle almond flour on all sides.
3. In a bowl, whisk cream of tartar and egg whites until they form stiff peaks.
4. In a pan, heat oil and sauté garlic and spinach for 4 minutes. Turn off the heat and stir in dried parsley.
5. In another pan, add coconut flour, almond milk, and black pepper. Whisk well and bring it to a boil, then simmer while whisking for 5 minutes. Let it cool.
6. Fold the sautéed spinach mixture, egg yolks, and Parmesan cheese into the cooled milk mixture and mix well.
7. Gently fold in the egg whites in batches.
8. Pour the mixture into the prepared ramekins, tap to remove excess air, and place them on a baking tray.
9. Bake for 5 minutes, then reduce the temperature to 350°F (180°C) and bake for an additional 20 minutes until soufflés are puffed and golden brown. Enjoy!

Nutrition Per Serving:

Calories - 152 | Fat - 6.5g | Carbs - 8g |
Protein - 14g | Sugar - 1g | Fiber - 2g |
Potassium - 249mg | Sodium - 182mg |
Cholesterol - 104mg

7.20 Huevos Rancheros

Preparation time - 15 minutes |
Cooking time - 25 minutes | Serves - 4
Ingredients:

- Onion, diced - ½ cup (80g)
- Tomatoes, fire-roasted, canned crushed - 15 oz. (425g)
- Water - 2 tbsp.. (30ml)
- Poblano pepper, diced - ½ cup (60g)
- Canola oil - 1 tsp. (5ml)
- Fresh jalapeño pepper - 1
- Garlic, minced - 1½ tsp. (4.5g)

For Huevos

- Avocado cut into quarters - 1
- Canola oil - 1 tsp. (5ml)
- Low-carb tortillas (6) - 4
- Eggs - 4
- Black soybeans, rinsed - 1 (15 oz.) can(425g)
- Cheddar cheese, shredded - ¼ cup (28g)

Procedure:

1. In a sizable pan, add oil and heat on medium flame, sauté your onion for about 2 minutes.
2. Mix in peppers and cook for 2 more minutes. Add in garlic. Continue cooking for an extra 1 minute.
3. Add water, salt and tomatoes, let it boil, reduce heat to low and let simmer for about 5 minutes. Take from heat and keep warm.
4. Using a skillet, add oil and cook egg for 4 minutes.
5. For each tortilla, add eggs and beans, tomato salsa, and the rest of the ingredients.
6. Roll and enjoy.

Nutrition Per Serving:

Calories - 307 | Fat - 17.5g | Carbs - 13g |
Protein - 19g | Sugar - 4.5g | Fiber - 5g |
Potassium - 458mg | Sodium - 128mg |
Cholesterol - 210mg

7.21 Eggplant Special

Preparation time - 15 minutes |
Cooking time - 1 h 40 min | Serves - 6
Ingredients:

- Eggs - 2
- Water - 2 tbsp. (30ml)
- Almond flour - 1 cup (100g)
- Fresh basil, torn - ¼ cup (10g)
- Eggplants sliced into ¼ thick slices - 2 pounds (907g)
- Italian seasoning - 1 tsp. (2g)
- Garlic cloves, minced - 2
- Black pepper - ½ tsp. (1.2g)
- Tomato sauce, unsalted - 1 (24 oz.) jar (680g)
- Red pepper flakes - ½ tsp. (0.6g)

Procedure:

1. Let your oven preheat to attain 400°F.
2. Oil spray a baking dish.
3. Using a bowl, add in egg and water and whisk.
4. Using a dish, combine Italian seasoning and almond flour.
5. Coat eggplant in whisked egg, then in bread crumbs, press to adhere.
6. Set breaded eggplant on the prepared baking sheet. Oil spray your eggplant on both sides.
7. Bake for half an hour, switch racks after flipping the eggplant in the upper and third rack.
8. Sprinkle pepper.
9. Using a bowl, add in garlic, tomato sauce, red pepper, and basil. Mix.
10. In the baking dish, add half a cup of the sauce, place the eggplant slices and add one cup of sauce on top.
11. Bake for 30 minutes, cool for about 5 minutes. Enjoy.

Nutrition Per Serving:

Calories - 203 | Fat - 9g | Carbs - 14g |
Protein - 12g | Sugar - 5.7g | Fiber - 7.5g |
Potassium - 583mg | Sodium - 217mg |
Cholesterol - 124mg

7.22 Zucchini Black Bean Tacos

Preparation time - 20 minutes |
Cooking time - 0 minutes | Serves - 4
Ingredients:

- Salsa, as needed

For tacos

- Chili powder - ½ tsp. (1g)
- Corn tortillas - 8
- Chipotle powder - ½ tsp. (1g)
- Black soybeans, rinsed - 1 (15 oz.) can (425g)
- Paprika - ¼ tsp. (0.6g)
- Garlic powder - ¼ tsp. (0.6g)
- Zucchini, grated - 1 med. sized

Avocado Crema (blend all ingredients)

- Greek yogurt, low-fat - ½ cup (160g)
- Avocado - 1 med. sized
- lime juice - of 1 lime

Procedure:

1. Using a bowl, add all the taco ingredients, except for tortillas.
2. Warm the tortillas in the oven.
3. Add the taco mix, salsa and avocado crema on top.
4. Enjoy.

Nutrition Per Serving:

Calories - 245 | Fat - 10g | Carbs - 15g |
Protein - 6g | Sugar - 1g | Fiber - 10g |
Potassium - 419mg | Sodium - 143mg |
Cholesterol - 8mg

7.23 Polenta Squares with Cheese & Pine Nuts

Preparation Time - 20 minutes + Cooling | Cooking Time - 40 minutes | Serves - 30
Ingredients -

- Quick-cooking polenta - 1 cup (160g)
- Gorgonzola cheese, low-fat, crumbled - ⅓ cup (38g)
- Unsalted butter - 1 tbsp. (14g)
- Boiling water - ¼ cup (60ml)
- Water - 4 cup (960ml)
- Balsamic vinegar - ⅔ cup (160ml)
- Toasted pine nuts - 3 tbsp. (25g)
- Flat-leaf fresh parsley, chopped - 2 tbsp. (8g)
- Grated zest - 1 tsp. (2g)
- currants - 3 tbsp. (30g)

Procedure:

1. In a pan, add water (4 cups) and boil; slowly add polenta while whisking, on low flame for 4 minutes till it thickens.
2. Add butter and pour in an oil sprayed baking pan (square-9).
3. Cover with plastic wrap on top; it should touch the polenta surface, keep in the fridge for 60 minutes. Slice in 30 squares.
4. In your bowl, mix currants with boiling water (1/4 cup). Let it rest for 10 minutes draining.
5. Using a bowl, add currants, zest, pine nuts, and cheese.
6. In a pan, add vinegar, cook on medium heat for ten minutes, until reduced by 2 tbsp. Let it cool.
7. Using a skillet set over a medium source of heat, add oil and heat. Mix in polenta squares and cook one side for 6 minutes.
8. Serve with cheese mixture and drizzle of vinegar.

Nutrition Per Serving:
Calories - 130 | Fat - 1.1g | Carbs - 18g | Protein - 3g | Sugar - 8mg | Fiber - 5g | Potassium - 300mg | Sodium - 201mg | Cholesterol - 40mg

8 VEGAN PLATES

8.1 Vegetarian Black Bean Pasta

Preparation time - 15 minutes |
Cooking time - 20 minutes | Serves - 6

Ingredients:

- Portobello baby mushrooms, sliced - 1¾ cup (245g)
- Olive oil - 1 tsp. (5ml)
- Tomatoes with juices, diced - 1 (15 oz.) can (425g)
- Garlic clove, minced - 1
- Black pepper - pinch
- Whole wheat fettuccine - 9 oz. (255g)
- Baby spinach - 2 cup (60g)
- Dried rosemary - 1 tsp. (1g)
- Black soybeans, rinsed - 1 (15 oz.) can (425g)
- Dried oregano - ½ tsp.(1g)

Procedure:

1. Cook the whole wheat fettuccine according to the package instructions.
2. In a skillet, set over medium heat, add olive oil and heat. Add mushrooms and sauté for 6 minutes.
3. Add minced garlic and continue cooking for 1 minute.
4. Mix in the diced tomatoes with juices, dried rosemary, and dried oregano. Toss well.
5. Add the cooked pasta, baby spinach, and rinsed black soybeans to the skillet. Toss to combine.
6. Serve and enjoy!

Nutrition Per Serving:
Calories - 255 | Fat - 3g | Carbs - 45g |
Protein - 12g | Sugar - 2g | Fiber - 14g |
Potassium - 399mg | Sodium - 113mg |
Cholesterol - 0mg

8.2 Lentil Medley

Prep Time - 20 minutes |
Cook Time - 25 min | Serves - 8

Ingredients:

- Water - 2 cup (480ml)
- Red onion, sliced - 1 med. Sized
- Mushrooms, sliced - 2 cup (290g)
- Lentils - 1 cup (190g)
- Potato, cubed - 1 med. Sized
- Tomato, soft, sun-dried - ½ cup (70g)
- Fresh mint - ¼ cup (10g)
- Olive oil - 3 tbsp.(45ml)
- Cucumber, cubed - 1 med. Sized
- Dried oregano - 1 tsp. (1g)
- Honey - 2 tsp. (10g)
- Rice vinegar - ½ cup (120ml)
- Baby spinach, chopped - 4 cup (120g)
- Dried basil - 1 tsp. (1g)

Procedure:

1. After rinsing, cook lentils in water until soft. Use cold water for draining and rinsing once again.
2. Transfer to a mixing bowl, mix in the remaining ingredients, toss and serve.

Nutrition Per Serving:
Calories - 225 | Fat - 8g | Carbs - 29g |
Protein - 6g | Sugar - 36mg | Fiber - 32g |
Potassium - 2977mg | Sodium - 400mg |
Cholesterol - 1mg

8.3 Zucchini with Corn

Preparation time - 20 minutes |
Cooking time - 20 minutes | Serves - 6

Ingredients:

- Olive oil - 1 tbsp. (15ml)
- Onion, diced - ¼ cup (60g)
- Zucchinis cut into ¼ thick slices - 3 med. Sized
- Fresh corn kernels - 4 cup (960g)
- Black pepper - ¼ tsp. (1.25g)
- Garlic clove, minced - 1
- Fresh jalapeño, chopped without seeds - 1
- Salt - ⅛ tsp. (1g)

Procedure:

1. Set corn in water and boil, cook for 10 minutes on low, cover, then drain.
2. In hot oil, add onion and garlic. Sauté for 5 minutes before adding zucchini and cook for an extra 5 minutes.
3. Add jalapenos, pepper, corn and pepper, cook for ten minutes.
4. Turn the heat off and serve.

Nutrition Per Serving:

Calories - 202 | Fat - 5g | Carbs - 40g |
Protein - 7g | Sugar - 8mg | Fiber - 20g |
Potassium - 899mg | Sodium - 164mg |
Cholesterol - 0mg

8.4 Couscous with Beans & Vegetables

Preparation time - 20 minutes |
Cooking time - 20 minutes | Serves - 6

Ingredients -

- Onion, diced - 1 med. sized
- Red bell pepper, julienned - 1 med. sized
- Carrot, sliced - 1 med. sized
- Olive oil - 2 tsp. (10ml)
- Vegetable broth, low-fat - 1 cup (240ml)
- Zucchini cut into half-moons - 1 med. Sized
- Celery rib, sliced - 1
- Tomato, sliced - 1 med. Sized
- Garlic, minced - 1 tsp. (5g)
- Red kidney beans, rinsed - 2 (16 oz.) cans (907.2)
- Cubed sweet potato - 1 med. Sized
- Dried thyme - 1 tsp. (5g)
- Salt - ⅛ tsp. (1g0
- Ground cumin - 1 tsp. (5g)
- Parsley, minced - ¼ cup (60g)
- Paprika - ½ tsp. (2.5g)
- Cayenne - ⅛ tsp. (1g)
- Whole-wheat couscous - 1 cup (240g)

Procedure:

1. Using a skillet set on a medium source of heat, add oil and heat. Sauté all vegetables for 5 minutes before add in garlic and cooking for approximately 30 seconds.
2. Mix in the rest of the ingredients, except for couscous, let it come to a simple boil while on high heat setting, turn the heat to low intensity then allow for simmering to take place for 15 minutes.
3. Cook couscous as per pack's instruction. Serve the vegetables with fluffed couscous.

Nutrition Per Serving:

Calories - 330 | Fat - 2.5g | Carbs - 65g |
Protein - 16g | Sugar - 36mg | Fiber - 37g |
Potassium - 4029mg | Sodium - 241mg |
Cholesterol - 0mg

8.5 Roasted Kabocha with Wild Rice

Preparation Time - 20 minutes | Cooking Time - 2 hours| Serves - 4

Ingredients:

- Olive oil - ¼ cup (60ml)
- Chili powder - 1 tsp. (5g)
- Black pepper - ¼ tsp. (1.25g)
- Wild rice - ½ cup (120g)
- Kabocha squash - 3 pound (1360g)
- Pumpkin seeds - ½ cup (14.7g)
- Pomegranate seeds - ½ cup (14.7g)
- Chopped fresh parsley, - ¼ cup (7.08g)
- Lime juice - 1 tbsp. (15ml)
- Honey - 1 tsp. (5ml)
- Lime zest - 1 tsp. (5g)

Procedure:

1. Let the oven preheat to 375 F.
2. With a fork, pierce the squash all over and place it on a baking sheet with aluminium foil.
3. Allow to roast for about 80 minutes.
4. Cut the squash into 5-6 pieces lengthwise. Take the middle part out.
5. Season the squash with oil (1 tbsp.) and sprinkles of pepper; set on your baking sheet flesh side up.
6. Broil the squash for 5-7 minutes.
7. In a skillet, add pumpkin seeds and oil (1 tbsp.) and allow to cook for 3 minutes. Mix in honey and chili powder, and continue cooking for 30 seconds. Take them out on a plate and cool.
8. Using a pan, add in water (1½ cups), and let it boil. Add rice and let boil, turn heat to low and let simmer for 25 minutes while covered, drain.
9. Using a bowl, add rice, pumpkin seeds, zest, juice, parsley, oil (2 tbsp.), and toss well.
10. Serve with broiled squash on top.

Nutrition Per Serving:

Calories - 250 | Fat - 17.2g | Carbs - 22g | Protein - 6g | Sugar - 8g | Fiber - 8g | Potassium - 550mg | Sodium - 135mg | Cholesterol - 0mg

8.6 Acorn Squash & Coconut Creamed Greens Casserole

Preparation Time - 20 minutes | Cooking Time - 2 hours| Serves - 4

Ingredients:

- Coconut milk - 1 (15 oz.) can (443ml)
- Jalapeno without seeds, minced - ½ med. sized
- Grape seed oil - 2 tbsp. (30ml)
- Cornstarch - 1 tbsp. (5g)
- Ginger, chopped - 2 tbsp. (30g)
- Garlic cloves, minced - 4
- Black pepper - ¼ tsp. (1.25g)
- Lime juice - 1 tbsp. (15ml)
- Plum tomatoes, diced - 2 med. sized
- Sweet onion. chopped - 1 med. sized
- Light agave syrup - 1 tsp. (5ml)
- Tuscan kale, chopped - 10 cups (2400g)
- Ground cumin - 2 tsp. (10g)
- Acorn squash sliced into 1/8 of thickness - 1¼ pound (567g)
- Packed Swiss chard, chopped - 7 cup (1680g)

Procedure:

1. Preheat the oven to 425°F (220°C). Mix the cornstarch with coconut milk.
2. Add and heat grape seed oil. Sauté the onion for about 4 minutes.
3. Add garlic, ginger, jalapenos, and continue cooking for 2 more minutes.
4. Add tomatoes to the onion mixture. Cook for 2 minutes, then mix in cumin and cook for an additional 1 minute, then add kale and chard to the skillet and cook until wilted and the liquid evaporates.
5. Add agave syrup and the coconut milk-cornstarch mixture. And simmer for 3 minutes. Stir in lime juice. In a baking dish, add the creamed greens, then place the sliced acorn squash on top. Bake for 25-30 minutes. Enjoy!

Nutrition Per Serving:

Calories - 248 | Fat - 17.2g | Carbs - 19g | Protein - 9g | Sugar - 4g | Fiber - 6.5g | Potassium - 835mg | Sodium - 124mg | Cholesterol - 0mg

8.7 Warm Spiced Cabbage Bake

Preparation Time - 20 minutes |
Cooking Time - 60 minutes| Serves - 4

Ingredients:

- raisins - 2 tbsp. (24g)
- Black pepper - ¼ tsp. (0.6g)
- Fresh dill, chopped - ½ cup (7.5g)
- Pine nuts, toasted - ⅓ cup (40g)
- Olive oil - 5 tbsp. (75ml)
- Savoy cabbage (6 wedges) - 1½ pounds (680g)
- Sweet onion, chopped - 1 med. sized
- Garlic cloves - 4
- Whole tomatoes, peeled & crushed - 1 (15 oz.) can (425g)
- Al l spice - A pinch (1g)
- Sweet paprika - 1 tsp. (2g)
- Low-fat vegan Sour cream - ½ cup (120g)
- Ground cinnamon - ¼ tsp. (0.6g)
- Red pepper flakes - ¼ tsp. (0.5g)
- Salt - a pinch (1g)

Procedure:

1. Let your oven preheat to attain 400°F.
2. Using a bowl, add dill, nuts and raisins and mix together.
3. Add 2 tbsp. of oil. Cook cabbage wedges for 5-6 minutes on both sides, take it out on a plate and sprinkle black pepper.
4. Add the remaining oil in the skillet, sauté garlic and onion on low flame for 4 minutes.
5. Mix in spices and continue cooking for 1 more minute.
6. Mix in water (1 cup) and tomatoes, add the nut mixture (half). Let it simmer and add salt to season.
7. Add your cabbage wedges to skillet and set in oven before baking for half an hour.
8. Serve with the rest of the nut mixture and sour cream topping.

Nutrition Per Serving:
Calories - 131|Fat - 3g | Carbs - 6g |
Protein - 21g |Sugar - 8mg | Fiber - 30g |
Potassium - 2115mg | Sodium - 145mg |
Cholesterol - 0mg

8.8 Curried Cauliflower with Chickpeas

Preparation Time - 20 minutes |
Cooking Time - 75 minutes| Serves - 4

Ingredients:

- Chickpeas, rinsed - ¾ cup (150g)
- Ginger, minced - 2 tbsp. (30g)
- Canola oil - 2 tsp. (10ml)
- Onion, chopped - 1 med. sized
- Water - 3 cup (720ml)
- Cauliflower broken into florets - 1 medium head
- Red bell pepper, diced - 1 med. sized
- Garlic cloves - 3
- Curry powder - 2 tbsp. (16g)
- Salt - ⅛ tsp. (0.6g)
- Vegetable broth, low-sodium - 1½ cup (360ml)

Procedure:

1. Cook chickpeas in a pressure cooker with water for 45 minutes on high pressure.
2. Let the pressure release naturally for 15 minutes, drain.
3. Sauté onion in hot oil for 3 minutes, add bell pepper and cook for 3 more minutes.
4. Mix in ginger and garlic, cook for 30 seconds.
5. In the pressure cooker, add cauliflower, salt, broth and curry powder. Add chickpeas with sautéed vegetables, cook on high pressure setting for 3 minutes. Release pressure quickly. Serve.

Nutrition Per Serving:
Calories - 224 | Fat - 6g | Carbs - 37g |
Protein - 11g | Sugar - 10mg | Fiber - 30g |
Potassium - 1865mg | Sodium - 201mg |
Cholesterol - 0mg

9 SIDES AND SMALL PLATES

9.1 Soy Sauce Green Beans

Preparation Time - 10 minutes |
Cooking Time - 2 hours | Serves - 12

Ingredients:

- Olive oil - 3 tbsp. (45ml)
- Green beans - 16 oz. (454g)
- Garlic powder - ½ tsp. (1.4g)
- Coconut sugar - ½ cup (100g)
- Low-sodium soy sauce - 1 tsp. (5ml)

Procedure:

1. Using a slow cooker, add in soy sauce,green beans, sugar, oil, and garlic powder. Mix well before covering and allowing to cook for 2 hours on low.
2. Toss well before dividing in serving plates and enjoy your side dish.

Nutrition Per Serving:

Calories - 46 | Fat - 4g | Carbs - 4g |
Protein - 1g | Sugar - 1mg | Fiber - 0g |
Potassium - 80mg | Sodium - 29mg |
Cholesterol - 0mg

9.2 Sour Cream Green Beans

Preparation Time - 10 minutes |
Cooking Time - 4 hours \ Serves - 8

Ingredients:

- Green beans - 15 oz. (425g)
- Corn - 14 oz. (397g)
- Mushrooms, sliced - 4 oz. (113g)
- Cream of mushroom soup, low-fat and sodium-free - 11 oz (312g)
- Low-fat sour cream - ½ cup (120g)
- Almonds, chopped - ½ cup (60g)
- Low-fat cheddar cheese, shredded - ½ cup (56g)

Procedure:

1. Using a slow cooker, add in all ingredients and mix. Toss well and cook for 4 hours on low setting while covered.
2. Stir again one extra time. Set in serving plates and enjoy.

Nutrition Per Serving:

Calories - 360 | Fat - 12.7g | Carbs - 58g |
Protein - 14g | Sugar - 10mg | Fiber - 0g |
Potassium - 967mg | Sodium - 220mg |
Cholesterol - 14mg

9.3 Cumin Brussels Sprouts

Preparation Time - 10 minutes |
Cooking Time - 3 hours | Serves - 4

Ingredients:

- Low-sodium veggie stock - 1 cup (240ml)
- Brussels sprouts, trimmed and halved - 1 pound (454g)
- Rosemary, dried - 1 tsp. (1g)
- Cumin, ground - 1 tsp. (2.3g)
- Mint, chopped - 1 tbsp.

Procedure:

1. Using a slow cooker, combine all the above ingredients. Set a lid in place and cook for 3 hours on low.
2. Divide in serving plates and enjoy your side dish.

Nutrition Per Serving:

Calories - 56 | Fat - 1g | Carbs - 11g | Protein - 4g | Sugar - 3mg | Fiber - 5g | Potassium - 460mg | Sodium - 65mg | Cholesterol - 0mg

9.4 Peach And Carrots

Preparation Time - 10 minutes |
Cooking Time - 6 hours | Serves - 6

Ingredients:

- Small carrots, peeled - 2 pound (907g)
- Cinnamon powder - ½ tsp. (1g)
- Low-fat butter, melted - ½ cup (11.35g)
- Peach, canned, unsweet - ½ cup (120g)
- Cornstarch - 2 tbsp. (16g)
- Stevia - 3 tbsp. (36g)
- Water - 2 tbsp. (30ml)
- Vanilla extract - 1 tsp. (5g)
- Ground nutmeg - A pinch (0.5g)

Procedure:

1. Using a slow cooker, mix in all the above ingredients. Toss well before you cover and cook for 6 hours on low.
2. Toss again one more time before setting in serving plates and enjoy your side dish.

Nutrition Per Serving:

Calories - 139 | Fat - 11g | Carbs - 35g | Protein - 4g | Sugar - 7mg | Fiber - 4g | Potassium - 25mg | Sodium - 199mg | Cholesterol - 0mg

9.5 Chive & Garlic Mash

Preparation Time - 8 minutes |
Cooking Time - 20 minutes | Serves - 2

Ingredients:

- Vegetable stock - 2 cup (480ml)
- Yukon potatoes, peeled - 2 pound (907g)
- Garlic cloves - 4
- Almond milk - ½ cup (120ml)
- Flavored vinegar - ½ tsp. (2.5g)
- Chives, chopped - ¼ cup (12g)

Procedure:

1. Using an instant pot, add in potatoes,garlic and broth.
2. Cook for 9 minutes on HIGH pressure setting while the lid is locked.
3. Naturally release pressure for about 10 minutes
4. Drain and keep the appropriate liquid that will maintain the required consistency.
5. You then mash your potatoes. Add in milk, chives and vinegar as you stir.
6. Enjoy!

Nutrition Per Serving:

Calories - 292 | Fat - 15g | Carbs - 34g | Protein - 7g | Sugar - 1g | Fiber - 4g | Potassium - 1230mg | Sodium - 410mg | Cholesterol - 0mg

9.6 Spiced Broccoli Florets

Preparation Time - 10 minutes |
Cooking Time - 3 hours | Serves - 10

Procedure:

- Broccoli florets - 6 cup (360g)
- Low-fat shredded cheddar cheese - 1½ cup (170g)
- Cider vinegar - ½ tsp. (2.5g)
- Yellow onion, chopped - ¼ cup (40g)
- Tomato sauce, sodium-free - 10 oz. (285g)
- Olive oil - 2 tbsp. (30ml)
- Black pepper - A pinch (0.5g)

Procedure:

1. Apply oil to your slow cooker for greasing. Mix in vinegar, broccoli, black pepper, tomato sauce and onion. Cook on high setting for 2½ hours on high while covered.
2. Sprinkle cheese over your mixture, cover again and let cook for 30 more minutes on high. Set in serving plates and enjoy your side dish.

Nutrition Per Serving:

Calories - 119 | Fat - 9g | Carbs - 6g | Protein - 6g | Sugar - 2mg | Fiber - 2g | Potassium - 288mg | Sodium - 272mg | Cholesterol - 18mg

9.7 Mashed Cauliflower with Garlic

Preparation Time - 5 minutes |
Cooking Time - 25 minutes | Serves - 4

Ingredients:

- Non-hydrogenated soft-bowl margarine - 1 tbsp. (14g)
- Cauliflower - 1 head med. sized
- Leek split into 4 parts, white only - 1 med. sized
- Garlic clove - 1
- Pepper - ¼ tsp. (0.6g)

Procedure:

1. Break up little bits of cauliflower. Steam the garlic, leeks, and cauliflower in water in a saucepan until they become tender for 25 minutes.
2. Using a food processor, add the vegetables and puree well to get a mashed potato-like texture. You can process in small portions at a given time.
3. Using a mixer if you want a finer finish. With a dishtowel, make sure to tightly keep the blender cap on. If the vegetables tend to be dusty, add some more hot water.
4. As per your taste, stir in margarine and pepper. Just serve.

Nutrition Per Serving:

Calories - 67 | Fat - 5g | Carbs - 4g |
Protein - 2g | Sugar - 2g | Fiber - 2g |
Potassium - 276mg | Sodium - 25mg |
Cholesterol - 0mg

9.8 Chinese-Style Asparagus

Preparation Time - 15 minutes |
Cooking Time - 4 minutes | Serves - 2

Ingredients:

- Water - ½ cup (120ml)
- Soy sauce, reduced-sodium - 1 tsp.(5ml)
- Sugar - ½ tsp.(2.5g)
- Fresh asparagus, remove woody ends and slice into 1½ inch pieces - 1½ pounds (680g)

Procedure:

1. Using a saucepan set over a medium high source of heat, mix in soy sauce, sugar and water and heat. Allow to get to boiling point before adding asparagus. Lower the heat intensity and let boil on low for 4 minutes until the asparagus becomes crispy and tender.
2. Set in serving bowls to serve.

Nutrition Per Serving:

Calories - 260 | Fat - 5g | Carbs - 20g |
Protein - 22g | Sugar - 0mg | Fiber - 0g |
Potassium - 695mg | Sodium - 89mg |
Cholesterol - 0mg

9.9 Fresh Fruit Kebabs

Preparation Time - 35 minutes |
Cooking Time - 0 minutes | Serves - 8

Ingredients:

- Low-fat lemon yogurt, sugar-free - 6 oz. (170g)
- Lime juice, fresh - 1 tsp. (5ml)
- Pineapple chunks each ½ inch in size - 4
- Red grapes - 4
- Lime zest - 1 tsp. (2g)
- Strawberries - 4 med. sized
- Kiwi, peeled and quartered - 1
- Banana, sliced into 4 ½ chunks - ½ med. sized
- Wooden skewers - 4

Procedure:

1. Using a shallow dish, add in lime zest, lime juice, and yogurt and whisk. Set in your refrigerator while covered until when ready for use.
2. To each of the skewers, thread each fruit. Serve alongside your lemon-lime dip.

Nutrition Per Serving:

Calories - 27 | Fat - 10g | Carbs - 20g | Protein - 10g | Sugar - 26mg | Fiber - 8g | Potassium - 138mg | Sodium - 3mg | Cholesterol - 0mg

9.10 Pomegranate & Ricotta Bruschetta

Preparation Time - 12 minutes |
Cooking Time - 12 minutes | Serves - 8

Ingredients:

- Lemon zest, grated - ½ tsp. (1.5g)
- Wholegrain nut bread slices - 6
- Ricotta cheese low fat - 1 cup (245g)
- Pomegranate arils - ½ cup (87.5g)
- Fresh thyme - 2 tsp. (0.7g)

Procedure:

1. Toast your bread to brown lightly.
2. In the meantime, use a bowl to whisk lemon zest and cheese.
3. Slice halfway the toasted bread. Spread cottage cheese to the top.
4. Add a topping of pomegranate and thyme.
5. Enjoy.

Nutrition Per Serving:

Calories - 69 | Fat - 1g | Carbs - 11g | Protein - 4g | Sugar - 18mg | Fiber - 16g | Potassium - 427mg | Sodium - 123mg | Cholesterol - 98mg

9.11 Carrot Sticks with Onion & Sour Cream

Preparation Time - 10 minutes |
Cooking Time - 0 minutes | Serves - 8

Ingredients:

- Carrot sticks - 2 cup (128g)
- Sweet onion, peeled and minced - 1
- Mayonnaise low fat - 2 tbsp. (15g)
- Sour cream - ½ cup (120g)
- Stalks celery, chopped - 4

Procedure:

1. Using a bowl, add in mayonnaise and sour cream. Whisk well to combine.
2. Add in onion and stir.
3. Set in the refrigerator for 1 hour and enjoy with carrot sticks and celery.

Nutrition Per Serving:

Calories - 60 | Fat - 3.1g | Carbs - 7.2g | Protein - 1.6g | Sugar - 10mg | Fiber - 15.6g | Potassium - 577mg | Sodium - 38mg | Cholesterol - 30mg

9.12 Parsley Fennel

Preparation Time - 10 minutes|
Cooking Time - 2h 30 minutes| Serves - 4

Ingredients:

- Avocado oil - 2 tsp. (5ml)
- Fennel bulbs, sliced - 2
- Turmeric powder - ½ tsp. (1.5g)
- Parsley, chopped - 1 tbsp. (3g)
- Juice and zest of 1 lime
- Veggie stock, low-sodium - ¼ cup (60ml)

Procedure:

1. In your slow cooker, add in and mix all the above ingredients and let cook for 2 ½ hours on LOW setting while covered.
2. Enjoy your side dish.

Nutrition Per Serving:

Calories - 47 | Fat - 1g | Carbs - 11g |
Protein - 2g | Sugar - 0.4mg | Fiber - 4g |
Potassium - 521mg | Sodium - 71mg |
Cholesterol - 0mg

9.13 Parsley Red Potatoes

Preparation Time - 10 min |
Cooking Time - 6 hours| Serves - 8

Ingredients:

- Baby red potatoes, halved - 16
- Olive oil - 2 tbsp. (30ml)
- Chicken stock, low-sodium - 2 cup (480ml)
- Carrot, sliced - 1 med. sized
- Yellow onion, chopped - ¼ cup (40g)
- Celery rib, chopped - 1
- Black pepper - A pinch (0.5g)
- Parsley, chopped - 1 tbsp. (3g)
- Garlic clove, minced - 1

Procedure:

1. Using a slow cooker, add in potatoes, carrot, onion, garlic, black pepper, oil, stock, celery, and parsley. Toss well and cook for 6 hours on low setting while covered.
2. Set in serving plates and enjoy your side dish.

Nutrition Per Serving:

Calories - 256 | Fat - 10g | Carbs - 44g |
Protein - 4.5g | Sugar - 4.7mg | Fiber - 4.5g |
Potassium - 48mg | Sodium - 846mg |
Cholesterol - 0mg

9.14 Italians Style Mushroom Mix

Preparation Time - 5 minutes |
Cooking Time - 25 minutes| Serves - 6
Ingredients:

- Mushrooms, sliced - 1 pound (454g)
- Italian seasoning - 1 tsp. (2g)
- Olive oil - 3 tbsp. (45ml)
- Tomato sauce with no-salt-added - 1 cup (240ml)
- Yellow onion, chopped - 1 med. sized

Procedure:

1. Mix the mushrooms with the oil, onion, Italian seasoning and tomato sauce, toss well, and allow to cook for 25 minutes while covered
2. Set in serving plates and enjoy your side dish.

Nutrition Per Serving:

Calories - 96 | Fat - 8g | Carbs - 7g |
Protein - 3g | Sugar - 3.9mg | Fiber - 1.8g |
Potassium - 403mg | Sodium - 219mg |
Cholesterol - 1mg

9.15 Honey sage carrots

Preparation Time - 27 minutes |
Cooking Time - 8 minutes| Serves - 4
Ingredients:

- Carrots, sliced - 2 cup (128g)
- Black pepper, ground - ¼ tsp. (0.6g)
- Butter - 2 tsp. (10g)
- Honey - 2 tbsp. (30g)
- Fresh sage, chopped - 1 tbsp. (3g)
- Salt - ⅛ tsp. (0.6g)

Procedure:

1. Load a medium saucepan with water and allow to boil. Mix in carrots and cook for 5 minutes until tender. Drain excess water and place aside.
2. A medium sauté pan is preheated, and butter is added. Add the carrots, sugar, sage, pepper, and salt until the pan is heated and the butter is melting. Sauté for approximately 3 minutes, stirring regularly. Enjoy.

Nutrition Per Serving:

Calories - 217 | Fat - 5g | Carbs - 7g |
Protein - 4g | Sugar - 12mg | Fiber - 8g |
Potassium - 460mg | Sodium - 94mg |
Cholesterol - 1mg

10 POULTRY RECIPES

10.1 Turkey with Spring Onions

Preparation Time - 10 minutes |
Cooking Time - 20 minutes | Serves - 4

Ingredients:

- Black peppercorns - ½ tsp. (1g) (adjust to taste)
- Turkey breast, boneless & skinless, sliced - 1 pound (454g)
- Water - 1 cup (240ml)
- Salt - pinch (2g) (adjust to taste)
- Spring onions, chopped - 2 tbsp. (16g)
- Tomatoes, cubed - 2 med. sized
- Olive oil - 1 tbsp. (15ml)

Procedure:

1. Using a pan set over medium-high heat, add olive oil and heat it.
2. Add chopped spring onions and cook for about 2 minutes until they become tender.
3. Mix in the cubed turkey breast and cook until the turkey is browned on all sides.
4. Add the crushed black peppercorns and cubed tomatoes to the pan and stir well.
5. Pour in the water and bring the mixture to a gentle simmer. Cover the pan and cook for about 15 minutes or until the turkey is fully cooked and tender.
6. Season with a pinch of salt to taste.
7. Serve the turkey with spring onions over a bed of brown rice or steamed vegetables for a wholesome and nutritious meal.

Nutrition Per Serving:

Calories - 179 | Fat - 6g | Carbs - 8g |
Protein - 23g | Sugar - 4mg | Fiber - 2g |
Potassium - 501mg | Sodium - 75mg |
Cholesterol - 65mg

10.2 Chicken with Tomatoes and Celery Stalk

Preparation Time - 10 minutes |
Cooking Time - 30 minutes|] Serves - 4

Ingredients:

- Chicken breast, skinless & boneless, cubed - 2 pounds (908g)
- Celery stalk, chopped - 1 med. sized
- Tomato, cubed - 1 med. sized
- Red onions, sliced - 2 med. sized
- Garlic, minced - 1 tsp.(3g)
- Zucchini, cubed - 1 med. sized
- Mushrooms - ½ cup (40g)
- Olive oil - 2 tbsp. (30ml)
- Black pepper - 2 tsp. (4g) (adjust to taste)
- Water - 1 cup (240ml)
- Salt - pinch (2g)

Procedure:

1. In a pot, sauté the red onions, garlic, and celery in olive oil until they become translucent and fragrant.
2. Add in the cubed zucchini and mushrooms and let them simmer for 2 minutes.
3. Then, add the cubed tomatoes and continue to sauté for another 2 minutes.
4. Add the chicken cubes and black pepper, and cook over medium heat for about 5 minutes, stirring occasionally.
5. Pour in the water and bring the mixture to a gentle simmer. Cover the pot and let it cook for about 20 minutes or until the chicken is fully cooked and tender.
6. Season with salt to taste, serve the chicken with tomatoes and celery stalk over a bed of brown rice or quinoa for a complete and healthy meal.

Nutrition Per Serving:

Calories - 265 | Fat - 7g | Carbs - 9.5g |
Protein - 38g | Sugar - 4mg | Fiber - 2g |
Potassium - 785mg | Sodium - 125mg |
Cholesterol - 101mg

10.3 Chicken Bowl with Red Cabbage

Preparation Time - 10 minutes |
Cooking Time - 20 minutes | Serves - 4
Ingredients:

- Sweet paprika - 1 tsp. (2g)
- Boiled chicken breast, skinless & boneless, sliced - 1 pound (454g)
- Carrots, peeled and grated - 2 med. sized
- Low-fat yogurt - ⅓ cup (80g)
- Red cabbage head, shredded & sautéed - 1 med. sized
- Black pepper - ½ tsp. (1g)
- Sesame seeds - pinch (1g)
- Lemon juice - 1 tbsp. (15ml)

Procedure:

1. In a medium-sized bowl, mix the chicken breast and grated carrots together.
2. Add the sweet paprika, low-fat yogurt, and sautéed red cabbage to the bowl.
3. Season with black pepper to taste and mix well until all ingredients are evenly combined.
4. Drizzle the lemon juice over the chicken bowl and sprinkle with sesame seeds.
5. Serve the chicken bowl with a side of brown rice or Quinoa for a complete and nutritious meal.

Nutrition Per Serving:
Calories - 261 | Fat - 5g | Carbs - 27g |
Protein - 29g | Sugar - 5mg | Fiber - 6g |
Potassium - 975mg | Sodium - 66mg |
Cholesterol - 73mg

10.4 Chicken Sandwich

Preparation Time - 10 minutes |
Cooking Time - 15 minutes | Serves - 4
Ingredients:

- Boiled chicken breast, skinless & boneless, sliced into 4 pieces - 5.3oz (150g) each
- Oregano, chopped - 1 tbsp. (1.5g)
- Cucumber, sliced - 1 med. sized
- Tomato, sliced - 1 med. sized
- Black pepper - 1 tsp (2g)
- Salt - to taste
- Low-fat yogurt - 4 tbsp.(60g)
- Low-fat cheddar cheese, shredded - 1 oz. (29g)
- Whole-wheat bread slices - 4

Procedure:

1. In a small bowl, mix the low-fat yogurt with chopped oregano to make the yogurt spread.
2. Marinate the chicken slices with a small amount of olive oil, black pepper, and a pinch of salt.
3. Heat a non-stick pan over medium heat and cook the chicken slices for about 2-3 minutes on each side until they are heated through.
4. Assemble the sandwiches by spreading the yogurt mixture evenly on 4 slices of whole-wheat bread.
5. Add a layer of sliced tomato, cucumber, and shredded low-fat cheddar cheese on top of the yogurt spread.
6. Place one piece of cooked chicken breast on each sandwich.
7. Top the sandwiches with the remaining slices of whole-wheat bread to complete them.
8. Serve immediately or pack for a healthy and delicious lunch option.

Nutrition Per Serving:
Calories - 265 | Fat - 9g | Carbs - 26g |
Protein - 25g | Sugar - 2mg | Fiber - 6g |
Potassium - 450mg | Sodium - 300mg |
Cholesterol - 47mg

10.5 Turkey and Zucchini Tortillas

Preparation Time - 10 minutes |
Cooking Time - 20 minutes | Serves - 4

Ingredients:

- Whole-wheat tortillas - 4
- Fat-free yogurt - ½ cup (120g)
- Turkey breast, cut into strips, boneless & skinless - 1 pound (454g)
- Olive oil - 1 tbsp. (15ml)
- Salt - ¼ tsp (1.5g) (adjust to taste)
- Pepper - ¼ tsp (1.5g) (adjust to taste)
- Oregano - ½ tsp (1g)
- Zucchini, sliced - 1 med. sized

Procedure:

1. Preheat the oven to 360°F (180°C).
2. In a mixing bowl, combine the turkey breast and zucchini with olive oil. Mix well to coat the turkey and zucchini with the oil.
3. Spread the mixture on a baking tray, sprinkle with salt, pepper, and oregano to taste.
4. Bake in the preheated oven for 20 minutes or until the turkey is fully cooked and zucchini is tender.
5. Warm the tortillas, place the cooked turkey and zucchini mixture on top and drizzle with fat-free yogurt.
6. Roll up the tortillas and serve with low-sodium dip of your choice.

Nutrition Per Serving:

Calories - 260 | Fat - 5g | Carbs - 30g | Protein - 27g | Sugar - 2mg | Fiber - 5g | Potassium - 510mg | Sodium - 85mg | Cholesterol - 65mg

10.6 Chicken with Eggplants

Preparation Time - 10 minutes |
Cooking Time - 35 minutes | Serves - 4

Ingredients:

- Chicken breasts, skinless, boneless and cubed - 1 (454g)
- Red onion, chopped - 1 med. sized
- Olive oil - 2 tbsp. (30ml)
- Salt - ¼ tsp (1.5g) (adjust to taste)
- Pepper - ¼ tsp (1.5g) (adjust to taste)
- Cherry tomatoes, halved - 1 cup (150g)
- Eggplant, cubed - 1 med. sized
- Smoked paprika - ½ tsp. (1g)

Procedure:

1. Preheat the oven to 360°F (180°C).
2. In a mixing bowl, combine chicken breast with paprika and olive oil. Mix well to coat the chicken with the spice mixture.
3. Transfer the seasoned chicken to a baking tray, spreading it out evenly.
4. Add the onion, cherry tomatoes, and eggplant to the tray with the chicken, sprinkle with salt and pepper.
5. Bake in the preheated oven for 25 minutes or until the chicken is fully cooked and the vegetables are tender.
6. Serve with a side of brown rice or quinoa for a balanced meal.

Nutrition Per Serving:

Calories - 260 | Fat - 10g | Carbs - 15g | Protein - 31g | Sugar - 4mg | Fiber - 6g | Potassium - 620mg | Sodium - 75mg | Cholesterol - 73mg

10.7 Garlic Turkey

Preparation Time - 10 minutes |
Cooking Time - 25 minutes | Serves - 4

Ingredients:

- Olive oil - 1 tbsp. (15ml)
- Turkey breast, boneless, skinless and sliced - 1 pound (454g)
- Garlic cloves, minced - 5
- Onion - ½ med. Sized, finely chopped
- Salt - to taste
- Cherry tomato - 2-3
- White pepper - to taste
- Dried thyme - ½ tsp. (0.5g)
- Balsamic vinegar - 2 tbsp. (30ml)

Procedure:

1. Preheat the oven to 360°F (180°C).
2. In a baking dish, combine the sliced turkey breast with olive oil, garlic, onion, salt, cherry tomatoes, pepper, thyme, and balsamic vinegar. Mix everything together to ensure the turkey is coated with the seasonings.
3. Spread the turkey mixture out evenly in the baking dish.
4. Bake in the preheated oven for 25 minutes or until the turkey is fully cooked and tender.
5. Serve with a side of steamed vegetables or a green salad.

Nutrition Per Serving:

Calories - 170 | Fat - 8g | Carbs - 6g |
Protein - 20g | Sugar - 3mg | Fiber - 1g |
Potassium - 450mg | Sodium - 200mg |
Cholesterol - 58mg

10.8 Cheddar Turkey

Preparation Time - 10 minutes |
Cooking Time - 30 minutes | Serves - 4

Ingredients:

- Turkey breast, boneless, skinless and sliced - 1 pound (454g)
- Dried basil - ½ tsp. (1g)
- Ground cumin - ½ tsp. (0.5g)
- Olive oil - 2 tbsp. (30ml)
- Fat-free shredded cheddar cheese - 1 cup (120g)
- Lime juice - 1 tbsp. (15ml)

Procedure:

1. Mix turkey breast with olive oil, dried basil, cumin, and lime juice.
2. Set on a tray and let bake for 25 minutes.
3. Then top the turkey with cheddar cheese and continue cooking for additional 5 minutes.

Nutrition Per Serving:

Calories - 301 | Fat - 1g | Carbs - 7g |
Protein - 27g | Sugar - 10mg | Fiber - 1g |
Potassium - 487mg | Sodium - 1330mg |
Cholesterol - 78mg

10.9 Parsnip and Turkey Bites

Preparation Time - 10 minutes |
Cooking Time - 40 minutes | Serves - 4

Ingredients:

- Turkey breast, boneless, skinless and cubed - 1 pound (454g)
- Parsnip, peeled and cubed - 2
- Salt - ¼ tsp (1.5g) (adjust to taste)
- Red pepper flakes - 1 tsp. (2g)
- Avocado oil - 2 tbsp. (30ml)
- Ground cumin - 1 tsp. (2g)
- Parsley, chopped - 1 tbsp. (3g)
- Water - 1 cup (240ml)
- Canola oil - for frying

Procedure:

1. In a pan set over medium-high heat, add avocado oil and heat it.
2. Add the cubed turkey breast and sauté for about 5 minutes or until the turkey is lightly browned.
3. Mix in the parsnip and spices. Stir well.
4. Pour in the water. Cover the pan and let it cook over medium heat for about 20 minutes or until the turkey and parsnip are tender and fully cooked.
5. Let cool, mash the mixture and form balls, fry them in little oil and serve hot with any dip of choice.

Nutrition Per Serving:

Calories - 190 | Fat - 1g | Carbs - 17g |
Protein - 24g | Sugar - 3mg | Fiber - 4g |
Potassium - 670mg | Sodium - 230mg |
Cholesterol - 63mg

10.10 Nutmeg Chicken with Tender Chickpeas

Preparation Time - 10 minutes |
Cooking Time - 40 minutes| Serves - 4

Ingredients:

- Green bell pepper, sliced - 1
- Red bell pepper, sliced - 1
- Yellow bell pepper, sliced - 1
- Chickpeas, canned, drained and no-salt-added - 1 cup (240g)
- Water - 1 cup (240ml)
- Yellow onion, chopped - 1 med. sized
- Onion, chopped - 1 med. sized
- Turkey breast, boneless, skinless and cubed - 1 pound (454g)
- Ground nutmeg - 1 tsp. (2g)
- Coconut oil - 1 tsp. (5ml)

Procedure:

1. Using a pan set over a medium high source of heat, add in coconut oil and let heat. Mix in onion, bell peppers, and turkey, and allow to cook for about 10 minutes as you occasionally stir.
2. Mix in the rest of your ingredients. Allow to simmer to about 30 minutes.

Nutrition Per Serving:

Calories - 387 | Fat - 12g | Carbs - 41g |
Protein - 30g | Sugar - 0mg | Fiber - 11g |
Potassium - 905mg | Sodium - 1201mg |
Cholesterol - 49mg

10.11 Green Chilli Turkey

Preparation Time - 10 minutes |
Cooking Time - 30 minutes | Serves - 4

Ingredients:

- Turkey breast, boneless, skinless, and cubed - 1 pound (454g)
- Fresh green chilies, ground - 3 to 5 (adjust to taste)
- Onion, diced - 1 med. Sized
- Tomato, diced - 2 med. sized
- Salt - to taste
- Lemon juice - 1 tbsp. (15ml)
- Olive oil - 2 tbsp. (30ml)

For garnish

- Fresh parsley, chopped - ¼ cup (5g)
- Red onion, sliced - 1 med. Sized

Procedure:

1. Preheat the oven to 365°F (185°C).
2. In a mixing bowl, combine the cubed turkey breast with green chilies and salt. Mix well to coat the turkey with the spices.
3. Add the diced onion, diced tomato, lemon juice, and olive oil to the bowl. Mix everything together until the turkey is evenly coated.
4. Transfer the seasoned turkey to a baking tray, spreading it out in a single layer.
5. Bake in the preheated oven for 30 minutes or until the turkey is fully cooked and slightly browned.
6. Garnish with chopped fresh parsley and longitudinally sliced onions before serving.

Nutrition Per Serving:

Calories - 180 | Fat - 7g | Carbs - 8g |
Protein - 25g | Sugar - 3mg | Fiber - 2g |
Potassium - 440mg | Sodium - 90mg |
Cholesterol - 65mg

10.12 Hot Chicken Mix

Preparation Time - 10 minutes |
Cooking Time - 30 minutes | Serves - 4

Ingredients:

- Scallions, chopped - 4
- Olive oil - 1 tbsp. (15ml)
- Chicken breast, skinless, boneless, and sliced - 1 pound (454g)
- Ginger, grated - 1 tsp. (5g)
- Salt - pinch (2g)
- Fresh parsley - ¼ cup (5g)
- Oregano, dried - ½ tsp. (0.5g)
- Ground cumin - ½ tsp. (1g)
- Chili powder - 1 tsp. (2g)

Procedure:

1. Preheat the oven to 360°F (180°C).
2. In a mixing bowl, combine the sliced chicken breast with scallions, ginger, olive oil, dried oregano, cumin, chili powder, and salt. Mix well to coat the chicken with the spices.
3. Transfer the seasoned chicken mixture to a baking tray, spreading it out in a single layer.
4. Bake in the preheated oven for 30 minutes or until the chicken is fully cooked and slightly browned.
5. Serve with a side of mixed greens or vegetables for a wholesome meal.

Nutrition Per Serving:

Calories - 190 | Fat - 7g | Carbs - 4g |
Protein - 26g | Sugar - 0.4mg | Fiber - 2g |
Potassium - 590mg | Sodium - 75mg |
Cholesterol - 68mg

10.13 Mustard and Garlic Chicken

Preparation Time - 10 minutes |
Cooking Time - 35 minutes| Serves - 4

Ingredients:

- Chicken thigh, boneless and skinless - 1 pound (454g)
- Olive oil - 1 tbsp. (15ml)
- Salt - ¼ tsp (1.5g) (adjust to taste)
- Red pepper - 1 tsp. (2g) (adjust to taste)
- Turmeric - ½ tsp. (1g)
- Mustard paste - 2 tbsp. (30g)
- Garlic cloves, minced - 5
- Dried basil - ½ tsp. (0.5g)

Procedure:

1. Preheat the oven to 365°F (185°C).
2. In a mixing bowl, combine olive oil, mustard paste, minced garlic, and dried basil to create the marinade.
3. Rub the chicken thighs with the mustard mixture until they are evenly coated. Sprinkle with salt, red pepper, and turmeric.
4. Place the marinated chicken thighs in a baking dish.
5. Bake in the preheated oven for 35 minutes or until the chicken is fully cooked and reaches a safe internal temperature.
6. Serve with a side of steamed vegetables or green salad for a complete meal.

Nutrition Per Serving:

Calories - 230 | Fat - 10g | Carbs - 2g | Protein - 33g | Sugar - 0.2mg | Fiber - 1g | Potassium - 450mg | Sodium - 85mg | Cholesterol - 96mg

10.14 Boneless Chicken Curry

Preparation Time - 10 minutes |
Cooking Time - 25 minutes | Serves - 4

Ingredients:

- Avocado oil - 1 tbsp.(15ml)
- Chicken breast, boneless, skinless, and cubed - 1 pound (454g)
- Tomato diced - 1 med. sized
- Salt - ¼ tsp (1.25g)
- Dried oregano - 1 tsp (1.25g)
- Smoked paprika - 1 tsp. (2g)
- Onion powder - ¼ tsp. (0.5g)

Procedure:

1. In a mixing bowl, rub the cubed chicken breast with avocado oil, smoked paprika, and onion powder until the chicken is evenly coated with the spices.
2. Add the diced tomatoes and dried oregano to the bowl, and mix everything together.
3. Transfer the seasoned chicken and tomatoes to a pan.
4. Cook on medium-high heat until the chicken is fully cooked.
5. Serve with brown rice or Quinoa and a side of steamed vegetables for a complete meal

Nutrition Per Serving:

Calories - 220 | Fat - 2g | Carbs - 5g | Protein - 30g | Sugar - 2g | Fiber - 1g | Potassium - 480mg | Sodium - 150mg | Cholesterol - 68mg

10.15 Chicken with Tomatoes

Preparation Time - 10 minutes |
Cooking Time - 25 minutes | Serves - 4

Ingredients:

- Avocado oil - 2 tbsp. (30ml)
- Ground black pepper - 1 tsp. (2g)
- Chicken thighs - 1 pound (454g)
- Cherry tomatoes, halved - 1 cup (150g)
- Salt - pinch (2g)
- Fresh parsley - ¼ cup (2g)
- Garlic cloves, minced - 2

Procedure:

1. Mix avocado oil chicken thighs, and black pepper.
2. Preheat the oven to 365°F (185°C).
3. Cook on medium-high heat until the chicken is half cooked, add the halved cherry tomatoes and minced garlic on top.
4. Cook for a few more minutes or until the chicken is cooked through.
5. Garnish with chopped fresh parsley before serving.

Nutrition Per Serving:

Calories - 180 | Fat - 9g | Carbs - 5g |
Protein - 22g | Sugar - 2mg | Fiber - 1g |
Potassium - 500mg | Sodium - 70mg |
Cholesterol - 65mg

10.16 Basil Turkey

Preparation Time - 10 minutes |
Cooking Time - 25 minutes | Serves - 4

Ingredients:

- Olive oil - 1 tbsp. (15ml)
- big boneless, skinless, and cubed turkey breast - 1 pound (454g)
- Fresh parsley - ½ cup (15g)
- red pepper flakes - 1 tsp (2g)
- Salt - ¼ tsp. (1.5g)
- ginger paste - 1 tbsp. (15g)
- dried basil - 1 tsp. (1g)
- lemon juice - 1 tbsp. (15ml)

Procedure:

1. Preheat the oven to 365°F (185°C).
2. In a mixing bowl, combine the cubed turkey breast, lemon juice, dried basil, olive oil,ginger paste, red pepper flakes, salt, and black pepper. Mix well to coat the turkey evenly with the marinade.
3. Place the marinated turkey on a baking tray and spread it out in a single layer.
4. Bake in the preheated oven for about 25 minutes or until the turkey is cooked through and reaches a safe internal temperature.
5. Garnish with chopped fresh parsley before serving.

Nutrition Per Serving:

Calories - 150 kcal | Fat - 6g | Carbs - 2g |
Protein - 23g | Sugar - 0.3g | Fiber - 0.4g |
Potassium - 270mg | Sodium - 85mg |
Cholesterol - 62mg

11 RED MEAT DISHES

11.1 Pork with Cherry Tomatoes

Preparation Time - 15 minutes |
Cooking Time - 25 minutes | Serves - 4

Ingredients:

- Avocado oil - 1 tbsp. (15ml)
- Cherry tomatoes, halved - 1 cup (150g)
- Salt - pinch (2g)
- Apple cider vinegar - 2 tbsp. (30ml)
- Pork tenderloin, chopped - 4 oz. (450g)
- Paprika powder - 1 tsp. (2g)

Procedure:

1. Preheat the oven to 365°F (185°C).
2. In a mixing bowl, combine the olive oil, halved cherry tomatoes, pinch of salt, and apple cider vinegar. Mix gently.
3. Add the chopped pork tenderloin to the bowl and toss with the tomato mixture to coat the pork evenly.
4. Transfer the mixture to a baking tray or casserole dish.
5. Sprinkle paprika powder over the top.
6. Bake in the preheated oven for about 30 minutes or until the pork is fully cooked and the cherry tomatoes are softened.
7. Serve the delicious and nutritious Pork with Cherry Tomatoes and enjoy your DASH Diet-friendly meal!

Nutrition Per Serving:

Calories - 210 kcal | Fat - 9g | Carbs - 5g | Protein - 26g | Sugar - 2g | Fiber - 1g | Potassium - 506mg | Sodium - 116mg | Cholesterol - 92mg

11.2 Thyme Pork Skillet

Preparation Time - 10 minutes |
Cooking Time - 25 minutes | Serves - 4

Ingredients:

- Pork top loin, boneless, chopped - 1 pound (450g)
- Olive oil - 1 tbsp. (15ml)
- Yellow onion, chopped - 1 med. sized
- Dried thyme - 1 tbsp. (15ml)
- Ginger paste - 1 tbsp.
- Black pepper - 1 tsp. (2g)
- Low-sodium chicken or vegetable broth - 1 cup (240ml)
- Low-sodium tomato paste - 1 tbsp. (15ml)

Procedure:

1. Heat the olive oil, add the chopped onion and sauté for about 5 minutes or until the onion becomes translucent.
2. Add the chopped pork to the skillet and continue cooking for an additional 5 minutes or until the pork is lightly browned on all sides.
3. Stir in the dried thyme and ginger paste, ensuring the pork is coated evenly with the spices.
4. Pour in the low-sodium broth and add the tomato paste to the skillet. Stir well to combine all ingredients.
5. Reduce the heat to medium, cover the skillet, and let it simmer for about 15 minutes or until the pork is fully cooked and tender. Adjust the seasoning with salt and pepper if desired.
6. Once the pork is cooked through. Serve the Thyme Pork Skillet alongside some steamed vegetables or a side of brown rice for a balanced and delicious dash diet meal.

Nutrition Per Serving:

Calories - 274 kcal | Fat - 11g | Carbs - 5g | Protein - 37g | Sugar - 1g | Fiber - 1g | Potassium - 484 mg | Sodium - 104 mg | Cholesterol - 93 mg

11.3 Meat and Zucchini Mix

Preparation Time - 10 minutes |
Cooking Time - 30 minutes | Serves - 4

Ingredients:

- Beef, boneless, cubed - 2 pounds (900g)
- Olive oil - 2 tbsp. (30ml)
- Water - ¾ cup (180ml)
- Marjoram, chopped - 1 tbsp. (15g)
- Zucchini, roughly sliced - 2 med. Sized
- Tomato, diced - 1 med. sized
- Sweet paprika - 1 tsp. (2g)
- Salt - pinch (2g)

Procedure:

1. Preheat the oven to 365°F (185°C).
2. In a large baking tray or casserole dish, combine the beef, olive oil, water, chopped marjoram, tomato, zucchinis, sweet paprika, and a pinch of salt.
3. Gently mix all the ingredients in the tray, ensuring they are evenly coated with the seasoning.
4. Flatten the mixture to create an even layer in the tray.
5. Place the tray in the preheated oven and cook the meal for 30 minutes or until the pork is fully cooked and the zucchinis are tender.
6. Once cooked, remove the tray from the oven.

Nutrition Per Serving:

Calories - 359 kcal | Fat - 9g | Carbs - 6g | Protein - 61g | Sugar - 2g | Fiber - 2g | Potassium - 1289mg | Sodium - 166mg | Cholesterol - 166mg

11.4 Garlic Pork

Preparation time - 10 minutes |
Cooking time - 40 minutes | Servings - 4

Ingredients:

- Olive oil - 3 tbsp. (45ml)
- Pork chops - 2 pounds (900g)
- Sweet paprika - 2 tsp. (4g)
- Onion - 1 med. sized
- Potato, cubed - 2 med. sized
- Salt - pinch (2g)
- Garlic powder - 1 tsp. (2g)

Procedure:

1. In a small bowl, mix together the garlic powder, sweet paprika, and olive oil to form a paste.
2. Rub the spice paste over the pork rib chops, ensuring they are evenly coated.
3. Preheat the oven to 365°F (185°C).
4. Place the pork chops in a baking tray or casserole dish.
5. Add the finely chopped onion and cubed potatoes around the pork chops in the tray.
6. Sprinkle a pinch of salt over the ingredients.
7. Bake the pork in the preheated oven for 40 minutes or until the pork is cooked through and tender.
8. Once cooked, remove the tray from the oven, serve hot with potatoes on top.

Nutrition Per Serving:

Calories - 344 kcal | Fat - 24g | Carbs - 6g | Protein - 26g | Sugar - 3g | Fiber - 2g | Potassium - 431mg | Sodium - 73mg | Cholesterol - 95mg

11.5 Beef with Cauliflower Rice

Preparation Time - 10 minutes |
Cooking Time - 40 minutes | Serves - 4

Ingredients:

- Cauliflower rice - 2 cup (340g)
- Chopped beef top loin - 1 pound (450g)
- Olive oil - 1 tbsp. (15ml)
- Dried oregano - 1 tsp. (2g)
- Chopped tomato - 1 med. Sized
- Red pepper flakes - 2 tsp. (4g) (adjust to taste)
- Salt - 1 tsp. (2g) (adjust to taste)
- Ginger - 1 tbsp. (15g)
- Garlic - 5 cloves
- Water - ½ cup (120ml)

Procedure:

1. In a large bowl, mix the chopped beef top loin with olive oil and dried oregano until the meat is evenly coated.
2. Transfer the seasoned meat to a pot or deep skillet, add tomato, ginger and garlic.
3. Sprinkle the red pepper flakes and salt over the ingredients in the pot.
4. Pour in the water.
5. Close the pot with a lid and cook the meal over medium heat for 40 minutes or until the beef is fully cooked and tender and the cauliflower rice is softened.
6. Once cooked, remove the pot from the heat, serve with cauliflower rice.

Nutrition Per Serving:

Calories - 449 kcal | Fat - 15g | Carbs - 39g | Protein - 37g | Sugar - 5g | Fiber - 9g | Potassium - 512 mg | Sodium - 338 mg | Cholesterol - 98 mg

11.6 Cilantro Beef Meatballs

Preparation Time - 10 minutes |
Cooking Time - 30 minutes | Serves - 4

Ingredients:

- Almond flour - 3 tbsp. (45g)
- Olive oil - 2 tbsp. (30ml)
- Grated ginger - 1 tbsp. (15g)
- Garlic, minced - 3 cloves
- Paprika - 2 tsp. (4g)
- Low sodium tomato paste - 2 tbsp. (30g)
- Salt - 1 tsp. (4g)
- Minced beef - 2 pounds (900g)
- Red onion - 1 med. Sized
- Olive oil (for brushing) - 1 tbsp. (15ml)
- Dried and chopped cilantro - 1 tbsp. (3g)

Procedure:

1. In a large mixing bowl, combine the cilantro, minced beef, almond flour, minced ginger, minced garlic, paprika, low-sodium tomato paste, and salt. Mix well until all ingredients are evenly incorporated.
2. Form the mixture into meatballs of your desired size and set them aside.
3. Preheat the oven to 365°F (185°C) and brush a baking tray with olive oil.
4. Place the meatballs on the prepared tray, ensuring they are evenly spaced.
5. Bake the meatballs in the preheated oven for 30 minutes or until they are fully cooked and slightly browned on the outside.
6. Once cooked, remove the meatballs from the oven and let them cool slightly.

Nutrition Per Serving:

Calories - 502 | Fat - 22g | Carbs - 9g | Protein - 68g | Sugar - 0 mg | Fiber - 4g | Potassium - 1242 mg | Sodium - 291 mg | Cholesterol - 247 mg

11.7 Spiced Meat with Endives

Preparation Time - 10 minutes |
Cooking Time - 35 minutes | Serves - 4
Ingredients:

- Chopped pork tenderloin - 1 pound (450g)
- Cherry tomatoes, diced - 3
- Onion, chopped - 2 tbsp. (30g)
- Garlic cloves, minced - 3
- Water - 1 cup (240ml)
- Endives, trimmed (shredded) - 2
- Chili powder - 1 tsp. (2g)
- White pepper, ground - 1 tsp. (2g)
- Dried oregano - ½ tsp. (1g)
- Olive oil - 1 tbsp. (15ml)

Procedure:

1. In a mixing bowl, combine the pork tenderloin with olive oil, chili powder, white pepper, and oregano. Mix well until the meat is evenly coated with the spices.
2. In a saucepan, roast each side of the seasoned meat over medium heat for about 2 minutes or until lightly browned.
3. Cover the saucepan with a lid and simmer over low to medium heat for 30 minutes or until the meat is fully cooked and tender.
4. Add shredded endives to a pan, and heat until softened.
5. Serve spicy meat with endives on the sides while hot.

Nutrition Per Serving:
Calories - 288 | Fat - 12g | Carbs - 4g |
Protein - 34g | Sugar - 0 mg | Fiber - 1g |
Potassium - 517 mg | Sodium - 114 mg |
Cholesterol - 98 mg

12 DESSERTS

12.1 Almond & Walnut Cake

Preparation Time - 10 minutes |
Cooking Time - 25 minutes | Serves - 8

Ingredients:

- Almond flour - 3 cup (360g)
- Liquid stevia - 5 tbsp. (75g)
- Walnuts, chopped - ½ cup (60g)
- Baking soda - 2 tsp. (8g)
- Almond milk - 2 cup (240g)
- Coconut oil, melted - ½ cup (120ml)

Procedure:

1. Preheat the oven to 365°F (185°C). Grease a cake pan with a little coconut oil or use parchment paper to prevent sticking.
2. In a mixing bowl, combine almond flour, liquid stevia, almond milk, baking soda, and melted coconut oil. Stir well until a smooth batter forms.
3. Gently fold in the chopped walnuts into the batter, leaving some for topping.
4. Pour the cake batter into the prepared cake pan, spreading it evenly, top with remaining walnuts.
5. Bake in the preheated oven for about 25 minutes or until the surface of the cake is light brown and a toothpick inserted in the center comes out clean.
6. Remove the cake from the oven and let it cool in the pan for a few minutes before transferring it to a wire rack to cool completely.
7. Once the cake is completely cooled, slice it into 8 servings and serve.

Nutrition Per Serving:

Calories - 245 | Fat - 21g | Carbs - 8g | Protein - 6g | Sugar - 1g | Fiber - 3g | Potassium - 101 mg | Sodium - 164 mg | Cholesterol - 0 mg

12.2 Vanilla Apple Cake

Preparation Time - 10 minutes |
Cooking Time - 30 minutes | Serves - 4

Ingredients:

- Almond milk - 1 cup (240ml)
- Baking powder - 1 tsp. (5g)
- Vanilla extract - 1 tsp. (5ml)
- Coconut flour - ½ cup (60g)
- Green apples, cored, peeled and chopped - 2 med. Sized
- Cooking spray - for greasing

Procedure:

1. Preheat the oven to 365°F (185°C).grease a small baking dish or cake pan with cooking spray or line it with parchment paper for easy removal.
2. In a mixing bowl, combine the coconut flour, baking powder, vanilla extract, and almond milk. Mix well until a smooth batter forms.
3. Gently fold in the chopped green apples into the batter.
4. Transfer the apple mixture to the prepared baking dish, spreading it evenly.
5. Bake in the preheated oven for about 30 minutes or until the top is golden brown and a toothpick inserted in the center comes out clean.
6. Remove the cake, once the cake is completely cooled, slice it and serve.

Nutrition Per Serving:

Calories - 190 | Fat - 11g | Carbs - 20g | Protein - 3g | Sugar - 10g | Fiber - 7g | Potassium - 269 mg | Sodium - 127 mg | Cholesterol - 0 mg

12.3 Coconut & Cinnamon Cream

Preparation Time - 2 minutes |
Cooking Time - 0 minutes | Serves - 4

Ingredients:
- Coconut cream - 1 cup (240g)
- Coconut sugar - 2 tbsp. (30g)
- Cinnamon powder - 1 tsp. (2g)
- Unsweetened coconut flakes - 1 tbsp. (7g)

Procedure:
1. In a blender, combine the coconut cream, coconut sugar, and ground cinnamon. Blend well until the mixture is smooth and creamy, for about 30 seconds.
2. Transfer the coconut and cinnamon cream to serving bowls or glasses.
3. Sprinkle the unsweetened coconut flakes on top for garnish.

Nutrition Per Serving:
Calories - 180 | Fat - 11g | Carbs - 20g | Protein - 3g | Sugar - 10g | Fiber - 7g | Potassium - 270 mg | Sodium - 127 mg | Cholesterol - 0 mg

12.4 Strawberries & Coconut Bowls

Preparation Time - 10 minutes |
Cooking Time - 0 minutes | Serves - 4

Ingredients:
- Strawberries, chopped - 2 cup (320g)
- Coconut cream - 1 cup (240g)
- Coconut shred - ¼ cup (20g)
- Almonds, chopped - for garnish

Procedure:
1. In a mixing bowl, combine the coconut cream with the unsweetened coconut flakes.
2. Divide the coconut mixture into serving bowls or plates.
3. Top each bowl with the chopped strawberries and almonds.
4. Enjoy the refreshing and healthy dessert.

Nutrition Per Serving: Calories - 67 | Fat - 0.2g | Carbs - 13g | Protein - 2g | Sugar - 9g | Fiber - 1g | Potassium - 112mg | Sodium - 29mg | Cholesterol - 0.2mg

12.5 Cinnamon Plums

Preparation Time - 10 minutes |
Cooking Time - 10 minutes | Serves - 4

Ingredients:
- Plums, halved, stones removed - 1 pound (454g)
- Cinnamon powder - ½ tsp. (1g)

Procedure:
1. Preheat your oven to 365°F (185°C).
2. Place the halved plums on a baking tray and sprinkle ground cinnamon evenly over the plums.
3. Bake the plums for 10 minutes or until they are soft and slightly caramelized.
4. Serve warm as a delicious and healthy dessert.

Nutrition Per Serving:
Calories - 31 | Fat - 0.2g | Carbs - 8g | Protein - 0.2g | Sugar - 7g | Fiber - 0.3g | Potassium - 26mg | Sodium - 3mg | Cholesterol - 0mg

12.6 Baked Apples with Nuts

Preparation Time - 10 minutes |
Cooking Time - 20 minutes | Serves - 4

Ingredients:
- Green apples, cored - 4 med. sized
- Ground cinnamon - 1 tsp. (2g)
- Coconut oil - 1 tsp. (5ml)
- Nuts, chopped (almonds, walnuts, or pecans) - 2 oz. (56g)

Procedure:
1. Preheat your oven to 365°F (185°C). Place the halved green apples in a baking tray, cut side up.
2. Drizzle coconut oil evenly and sprinkle with ground cinnamon.
3. Spread the chopped nuts over the apples, pressing them gently to stick.
4. Bake the apples in the preheated oven for 20 minutes or until they are tender and slightly caramelized.
5. Serve warm as a delightful dessert.

Nutrition Per Serving:
Calories - 156 | Fat - 2g | Carbs - 33g | Protein - 2g | Sugar - 25g | Fiber - 5g | Potassium - 240mg | Sodium - 15mg | Cholesterol - 0mg

12.7 Green Tea and Banana Sweetening Mix

Preparation Time - 10 minutes |
Cooking Time - 5 minutes | Serves - 3-4
Ingredients:

- Coconut cream - 1 cup (240ml)
- Avocados, chopped - 2 med. Sized
- Bananas, chopped - 2 med. Sized
- Green tea powder - 2 tbsp. (10g)
- Palm sugar - 1 tbsp. (15g)
- Lime zest, grated - 1 tbsp. (3g)

Procedure:

1. In a blender or food processor, combine coconut cream, chopped avocados, chopped bananas, green tea powder, honey or maple syrup, and grated lime zest.
2. Blend the mixture until smooth and well combined.
3. Transfer the sweetening mix to an airtight container and refrigerate for at least 30 minutes before serving.
4. Serve the green tea and banana sweetening mix cold as a delicious and nutritious sweetener for various dishes.

Nutrition Per Serving:
Calories - 162 | Fat - 8g | Carbs - 20g | Protein - 2g | Sugar - 11g | Fiber - 4g | Potassium - 388mg | Sodium - 7mg | Cholesterol - 0mg

12.8 Grapefruit Compote

Preparation Time - 5 minutes |
Cooking Time - 8 minutes| Serves - 4
Ingredients:

- Palm sugar - 1 cup (200g)
- Sugar-free red grape fruit juice - 4 cup (960ml)
- Mint, chopped - ½ cup (10g)
- Grape fruits, peeled and cubed - 2 med. Sized (600g)

Procedure:

1. Take all ingredients and combine them into Instant Pot.
2. Cook for 8 minutes on Low setting, then divide into serving bowls and enjoy!

Nutrition Per Serving:
Calories - 103 | Fat - 0.2g | Carbs - 26g | Protein - 1g | Sugar - 18g | Fiber - 2g | Potassium - 328mg | Sodium - 7mg | Cholesterol - 0mg

12.9 Instant Pot Applesauce

Preparation Time - 10 minutes |
Cooking Time - 10 minutes| Serves - 8
Ingredients:

- Apples - 3 pounds (1361g)
- Water - ½ cup (120g)

Procedure:

1. Core, peel, and chop the apples into small pieces. Place them at the bottom of the Instant Pot and add water.
2. Secure the lid of the Instant Pot and ensure the vent is sealed. Cook on high pressure for 10 minutes.
3. Once the cooking is complete, perform a natural pressure release.
4. Blend until smooth using a blender or a food processor.
5. Store the apple sauce in clean, airtight jars in the refrigerator for future use or enjoy it immediately as a healthy and delicious snack or side dish.

Nutrition Per Serving:
Calories - 36 | Fat - 0.2g | Carbs - 10g | Protein - 0.2g | Sugar - 7g | Fiber - 2g | Potassium - 88mg | Sodium - 0.5mg | Cholesterol - 0mg

12.10 Rice and Fruits Pudding

Preparation Time - 10 minutes |
Cooking Time - 25 minutes | Serves - 4

Ingredients:

- Black rice, cooked - 1 cup (180g)
- Pears, cored and cubed - 2 med. sized
- Cinnamon powder - 2 tsp. (4g)
- Coconut milk - ½ cup(120g)

Procedure:

1. Preheat the oven to 350°F (180°C).
2. In a mixing bowl, combine the cooked black rice, cubed pears,ground cinnamon, and coconut milk. Mix well until all ingredients are evenly distributed.
3. Divide the mixture into individual baking ramekins.
4. Bake the pudding in the preheated oven for 25 minutes or the pudding is set.
5. Remove from the oven and let it cool slightly before serving, with your favorite topping.

Nutrition Per Serving:

Calories - 186 | Fat - 6g | Carbs - 30g | Protein - 2g | Sugar - 12g | Fiber - 5g | Potassium - 248mg | Sodium - 18mg | Cholesterol - 0mg

12.11 Rhubarb and Pear Compote

Preparation Time - 10 minutes |
Cooking Time - 15 minutes | Serves - 4

Ingredients:

- Rhubarb, roughly chopped - 2 cup (240g)
- Pears, chopped - 2 med. sized
- Water - 2 cup (480ml)

Procedure:

1. In a pot, combine the roughly chopped rhubarb, chopped pears, and water. Heat the mixture until it comes to a boil.
2. Reduce the heat and simmer the compote for 15 minutes or until the fruits are tender and the mixture has thickened slightly.
3. Remove the pot from the heat and let the compote cool well before serving.
4. Optionally, you can add a sweetener like stevia or honey if desired.

Nutrition Per Serving:

Calories - 54 | Fat - 0.2g | Carbs - 14g | Protein - 1g | Sugar - 7g | Fiber - 2g | Potassium - 246mg | Sodium - 1mg | Cholesterol - 0mg

12.12 Lime Cake

Preparation Time - 10 minutes |
Cooking Time - 35 minutes | Serves - 6
Ingredients:

- Whole wheat flour - 2 cup (240g)
- Coconut oil - 2 tbsp. (30g)
- Egg, whisked - 1
- Baking powder - 1 tsp. (5g)
- Coconut milk - 1 cup (240ml)
- Lemon, sliced - ½ med. sized lime

Procedure:

1. Preheat your oven to 360°F (180°C) and prepare a baking pan by greasing it lightly or lining it with parchment paper.
2. In a mixing bowl, combine the whole wheat flour, baking powder, melted coconut oil, whisked egg, and unsweetened coconut milk. Mix well until the batter is smooth and homogeneous.
3. Pour the cake batter into the prepared baking pan.
4. Arrange the sliced lime on top of the cake batter.
5. Bake the cake in the preheated oven for about 35 minutes or until a toothpick inserted into the center comes out clean.
6. Serve with cream topping or as you desire.

Nutrition Per Serving:
Calories - 210 | Fat - 9g | Carbs - 27g |
Protein - 5g | Sugar - 0.3g | Fiber - 4g |
Potassium - 121mg | Sodium - 125mg |
Cholesterol - 31mg

12.13 Coconut Shred Bars

Preparation Time - 10 minutes |
Cooking Time - 25 minutes | Serves - 6
Ingredients:

- Coconut flour - 1 cup (120g)
- Baking powder - 1 tsp. (5g)
- Nutmeg (ground) - ½ tsp. (1g)
- Coconut oil - ½ cup (120ml)
- Coconut shred - ½ cup (40g)
- Egg, whisked - 1

Procedure:

1. Preheat your oven to 380°F (190°C) and prepare a baking tray by greasing it lightly or lining it with parchment paper.
2. In a mixing bowl, combine the coconut flour, baking powder, ground nutmeg, melted coconut oil, unsweetened coconut shred, and whisked egg. Mix until you have a smooth and thick batter.
3. Pour the batter into the prepared baking tray and gently flatten it to even thickness.
4. Bake the bars in the preheated oven for about 25 minutes or until they are golden brown and firm to touch.
5. Once baked, remove the bars from the oven and let them cool in the tray for a few minutes before slicing them into bars.
6. Let the coconut shred bars cool completely before serving. Enjoy them cold.

Nutrition Per Serving:
Calories - 177 | Fat - 14g | Carbs - 9g |
Protein - 4g | Sugar - 1g | Fiber - 4g |
Potassium - 149mg | Sodium - 58mg |
Cholesterol - 31mg

12.14 Cocoa Squares

Preparation Time - 10 minutes |
Cooking Time - 20 minutes | Serves - 4

Ingredients:

- Peaches, chopped - 3 med. sized
- Baking soda - ½ tsp. (2.5g)
- Coconut flour - 1 cup (120g)
- Coconut oil - 4 tbsp. (60ml)
- Cocoa powder - 2 tbsp. (10g)

Procedure:

1. Preheat your oven to 375°F (190°C) and prepare a square baking pan by lining it with parchment paper or greasing it lightly.
2. In a blender, combine the chopped peaches, baking soda, coconut flour, melted coconut oil, and unsweetened cocoa powder. Blend until you have a smooth mixture.
3. Pour the mixture into the prepared square pan, spreading it evenly.
4. Bake the cocoa squares in the preheated oven for about 20 minutes or until a toothpick inserted into the center comes out clean.
5. Once baked, remove the pan from the oven and let the dessert cool.
6. Once cooled, cut the dessert into squares before serving.

Nutrition Per Serving:

Calories - 157 | Fat - 9g | Carbs - 19g |
Protein - 2g | Sugar - 10g | Fiber - 5g |
Potassium - 273mg | Sodium - 137mg |
Cholesterol - 0mg

13 SMOOTHIES RECIPES

13.1 Blueberry-Vanilla Yogurt Smoothie

Preparation Time - 5 minutes |
Cooking Tim - 0 minutes| Serves - 2

Ingredients:

- Blueberries (frozen) - 1½ cup (240g)
- Vanilla Greek yogurt, Non-fat - 1 cup (240g)
- Non-fat or low-fat milk - 1 cup (240ml)
- Banana, frozen, peeled and sliced - 1 med. sized
- Ice - 1 cup (240g)

Procedure:

1. In a blender, add all the ingredients. Blend well until you have a creamy and smooth consistency.
2. Enjoy immediately.

Nutrition Per Serving:

Calories - 186 | Fat - 1g | Carbs - 40g |
Protein - 11g | Sugar - 24g | Fiber - 5g |
Potassium - 517mg | Sodium - 63mg |
Cholesterol - 0mg

13.2 Peaches And Greens Smoothie

Preparation Time - 5 minutes |
Cooking Time – 0 | Serves - 2

Ingredients:

- Fresh spinach - 2 cup (60g)
- Frozen peaches (or fresh, pitted) - 1 cup (150g)
- Ice - 1 cup (240g)
- Low-fat or nonfat milk - ½ cup (120ml)
- Plain nonfat or low-fat Greek yogurt - ½ cup (120g)
- Vanilla extract - ½ tsp. (2.5ml)
- No-calorie sweetener of choice (Optional)

Procedure:

1. Add all of the components to a blender and process until smooth.
2. Enjoy immediately.

Nutrition Per Serving:

Calories - 105 | Fat - 1g | Carbs - 22g |
Protein - 5g | Sugar - 17g | Fiber - 3g |
Potassium - 376mg | Sodium - 36mg |
Cholesterol - 2mg

13.3 Banana Breakfast Smoothie

Preparation Time - 5 minutes |
Cooking Time - 0 minutes| Serves - 1

Ingredients:

- Frozen banana - 1 med. sized
- 1% low-fat milk - ½ cup (120ml)
- Honey - 1 tbsp. (15g)
- Vanilla yogurt, fat-free - 1 (6 oz.) carton (170g)
- Ice, crushed - ½ cup (120g)

Procedure:

1. In your blender, add all the ingredients. Pulse until smooth and creamy.
2. Pour into a glass to serve.

Nutrition Per Serving: Calories - 82 | Fat - 1g
Carbs - 47g |Protein - 7g | Sugar - 33g |
Fiber - 3g | Potassium - 487mg |
Sodium - 55mg | Cholesterol - 5mg

13.4 Chocolate Berry Smoothie

Preparation Time - 5 minutes|
Cooking Time - 0 minutes| Serves - 1

Ingredients:

- Cold water - 1½ cup (360ml)
- Frozen blueberries - ¼ cup (40g)
- Avocado - ½ med. Sized (40g)
- Cashews - 2 tbsp. (20g)
- Organic cocoa powder - 2 tbsp. (10g)
- Vanilla extract - ½ tsp. (2.5ml)

Procedure:

1. In your blender, add all the above ingredients.
2. Pulse on high setting until the mixture becomes smooth and creamy.
3. Pour into a glass and enjoy it.

Nutrition Per Serving:

Calories - 319 | Fat - 19g | Carbs - 31g | Protein - 6g | Sugar - 9g | Fiber - 11g | Potassium - 527mg | Sodium - 9mg | Cholesterol - 0mg

13.5 Tropical Turmeric Smoothie

Preparation Time - 5 minutes |
Cooking Time - 0 minutes| Serves - 1

Ingredients:

- Turmeric - ½ tsp. (1.5g)
- Almond milk - 1 cup (240ml)
- Ginger - ½ tsp. (1.5g)
- Banana - 1 med. Sized
- Olive oil - 1 tbsp. (15ml)
- Frozen mango - ½ cup (75g)
- Cinnamon - ½ tsp. (1g)

Procedure:

1. In your blender, mix in the above ingredients.
2. Pulse using the high-speed setting until the mixture becomes smooth and creamy.
3. Pour into a glass and serve.

Nutrition Per Serving:

Calories - 295 | Fat - 12g | Carbs - 45g | Protein - 4g | Sugar - 22g | Fiber - 6g | Potassium - 487mg | Sodium - 80mg | Cholesterol - 0mg

13.6 Carrot Juice Smoothie

Preparation Time - 5 minutes |
Cooking Time - 0 minutes | Serves - 1

Ingredients:

- Almond milk (unsweetened) - 1 cup (240ml)
- Ripe banana - 1 med. Sized
- Cinnamon - ½ tsp. (1g)
- Fresh ginger - ½ tbsp. (4g)
- Carrot juice - ½ cup (120ml)
- Frozen pineapple - 1 cup (150g)
- Ground turmeric - ¼ tsp. (0.5g)
- Lime juice - 1 tbsp. (15ml)

Procedure:

1. In your blender, add and mix the above ingredients.
2. Pulse using high speed until the mixture becomes smooth and creamy.
3. Serve in a glass.

Nutrition Per Serving:

Calories - 241 | Fat - 4g | Carbs - 53g | Protein - 3g | Sugar - 30g | Fiber - 8g | Potassium - 830mg | Sodium - 108mg | Cholesterol - 0mg

13.7 Mixed Berries Smoothie

Preparation Time - 5 minutes |
Cooking Time - 0 minutes| Serves - 2

Ingredients:

- Frozen blueberries - ¼ cup (40g)
- Frozen blackberries - ¼ cup (40g)
- Almond milk (unsweetened) - 1 cup (240ml)
- Vanilla bean extract - 1 tsp. (5ml)
- Flax-seeds - 3 tsp. (15g)
- Chilled Greek yogurt - 1 scoop (about 30g)
- Stevia (optional) - as needed

Procedure:

1. In a blender, mix everything and emulsify. Pulse the mixture until you have your desired thickness. Serve fresh.

Nutrition Per Serving:

Calories - 130 | Fat - 4g | Carbs - 19g | Protein - 7g | Sugar - 8g | Fiber - 6g | Potassium - 206mg | Sodium - 43mg | Cholesterol - 3mg

13.8 Satisfying Berry and Almond Smoothie

Preparation Time - 5 minutes |
Cooking Time - 0 minutes | Serves - 4
Ingredients:

- Whole banana - 1 med. Sized
- Blueberries (frozen) - 1 cup (150g)
- Almond butter - 1 tbsp. (15g)
- Almond milk - ½ cup (120g)
- Water - as needed

Procedure:

1. Add the listed ingredients to your blender and blend well until you have a smoothie-like texture.
2. If needed, adjust the consistency with water.
3. Chill and serve.
4. Enjoy!

Nutrition Per Serving:
Calories - 138 | Fat - 6g | Carbs - 20g |
Protein - 3g | Sugar - 9g | Fiber - 4g |
Potassium - 248mg | Sodium - 64mg |
Cholesterol - 0mg

13.9 Refreshing Mango and Pear Smoothie

Preparation Time - 5 minutes |
Cooking Time - 0 minutes| Serves - 1
Ingredients:

- Ripe mango, cored and chopped - 1 med. sized
- Pear, peeled, pitted and chopped - ½ med. sized
- Kale, chopped - 1 cup (67g)
- Plain Greek yogurt - ½ cup (120g)
- Ice cubes - 2

Procedure:

1. Add pear, mango, yogurt and kale to a blender and puree.
2. Add ice and blend well to obtain a mixture with a smooth texture.
3. Enjoy!

Nutrition Per Serving:
Calories - 244 | Fat - 4g | Carbs - 48g |
Protein - 12.5g | Sugar - 30g | Fiber - 7g |
Potassium - 949mg | Sodium - 48mg |
Cholesterol - 6mg

13.10 Blackberry and Apple Smoothie

Preparation Time - 5 minutes |
Cooking Time - 0 minutes| Serves - 2
Ingredients:

- Frozen blackberries - 2 cup (300g)
- Apple cider - ½ cup (120ml)
- Apple, cubed - 1 med. Sized
- Non-fat lemon yogurt - 2/3 cup (160g)

Procedure:

1. In a blender, add the above ingredients. Thoroughly blend well to obtain a smooth consistency.
2. Chill before serving.

Nutrition Per Serving:
Calories - 130 | Fat - 1g | Carbs - 30g |
Protein - 5g | Sugar - 19g | Fiber - 8g |
Potassium - 344mg | Sodium - 33mg |
Cholesterol - 2mg

13.11 Raspberry Green Smoothie

Preparation Time - 5 minutes |
Cooking Time - 0 minutes| Serves - 1
Ingredients:

- Raspberries - 1 cup (150g)
- Water - 1 cup(240ml)
- Spinach - ¼ cup (25g)
- Chia seeds - 1 tbsp. (15g)
- Lemon juice - 2 tbsp. (30ml)
- Banana - 1 med. Sized
- Almond butter - 1 tbsp. (15g)

Procedure:

1. Using a blender, add in all ingredients. Pulse well to get a creamy and smooth consistency.
2. Pour into a glass and enjoy.

Nutrition Per Serving:
Calories - 269 | Fat - 14g | Carbs - 38g |
Protein - 6g | Sugar - 14g | Fiber - 17g |
Potassium - 690mg | Sodium - 8mg |
Cholesterol - 0mg

13.12 Blueberry Smoothie

Preparation Time - 5 minutes |
Cooking Time - 0 minutes| Serves - 2

Ingredients:

- Spinach - 1 cup (30g)
- Pineapple - 2 cup (300g)
- Coconut water - 4 cup (240ml)
- Blueberries - 1 cup (150g)
- Apple - 1 med. Sized
- Watermelon - 2 cup (300g)

Procedure:

1. Using your blender, add in ingredients.
2. Pulse on high setting until you obtain a creamy and smooth consistency.
3. Pour into a glass and enjoy.

Nutrition Per Serving:

Calories - 114 | Fat - 0.5g | Carbs - 29g | Protein - 2g | Sugar - 20g | Fiber - 4g | Potassium - 463mg | Sodium - 38mg | Cholesterol - 0mg

13.13 Avocado Smoothie

Preparation Time - 5 minutes |
Cooking Time - 0 minutes| Serves - 1

Ingredients:

- Cacao powder - 2 tbsp. (10g)
- Avocado - ½ med. Sized
- Frozen banana - ½ med. Sized
- Chia seeds - ½ tsp. (2.5g)
- Plain almond milk - ¼ cup (60ml)
- Lime juice (optional) - 2 tbsp. (30ml)

Procedure:

1. In a blender, add the above ingredients. Process on high speed to get a creamy and smooth consistency.
2. Enjoy.

Nutrition Per Serving:

Calories - 243 | Fat - 15g | Carbs - 28g | Protein - 4g | Sugar - 10g | Fiber - 10g | Potassium - 573mg | Sodium - 73mg | Cholesterol - 0mg

13.14 Chocolate and Peanut Butter Smoothie

Preparation Time - 5 minutes |
Cooking Time - 0 minutes | Serves - 4

Ingredients:

- Unsweetened cocoa powder - 1 tbsp. (5g)
- Peanut butter - 2 tbsp. (32g)
- Banana - 1 med. Sized
- Matcha powder - 1 tsp. (2g)
- Unsweetened soy milk - 1 cup (240ml)
- Rolled oats - ¼ cup (40g)
- Flax-seeds - 2 tbsp. (14g)
- Maple syrup - 1 tbsp. (15ml)
- Water - 1 cup (240ml)

Procedure:

1. Add in the above ingredients to your blender, then process until creamy and smooth consistency is achieved. Add water or soy milk if necessary.
2. Serve fresh!

Nutrition Per Serving: Calories - 336 | Fat - 15g | Carbs - 40g | Protein - 11g | Sugar - 13g | Fiber - 9.5g | Potassium - 603mg | Sodium - 82mg | Cholesterol - 0mg

13.15 Ultimate Fruit Smoothie

Preparation Time - 5 minutes |
Cooking Time - 0 minutes| Serves - 1

Ingredients:

- Strawberries - 1 cup (150g)
- 2% milk - 1 cup (240ml)
- Mango, cut into chunks - ½ med. Sized
- Fresh peach sliced - ½ med. Sized
- Orange juice - 1 cup (240ml)
- Pineapple - ¼ cup (60g)

Procedure:

1. Using a blender, mix in strawberries, milk, mango chunks, peach slices, orange juice and pineapple. Blend well until smooth.
2. Add more milk if required and serve fresh.

Nutrition Per Serving: Calories - 150 | Fat - 2g | Carbs - 30g | Protein - 5g | Sugar - 21g | Fiber - 4g | Potassium - 400mg | Sodium - 30mg | Cholesterol - 2mg

13.16 Oat Cocoa Smoothie

Preparation Time - 5 minutes |
Cooking Time - 0 minutes| Serves - 1

Ingredients:

- Vanilla extract - 1 tsp. (5ml)
- Skim milk - 1½ cup (360ml)
- Plain low-fat yogurt - 1 cup (240g)
- Ground flax-seeds - 2 tbsp. (14g)
- Banana - 1 med. Sized
- Unsweetened cocoa powder - 2 tbsp. (10g)
- Quick-cook oats - ½ cup (40g)
- Ground cinnamon - a dash

Procedure:

1. Place all ingredients in your blender. Process well to obtain a smooth consistency. Add more milk if required.
2. Enjoy.

Nutrition Per Serving:

Calories - 180 | Fat - 3g | Carbs - 35g |
Protein - 8g | Sugar - 12g | Fiber - 6g |
Potassium - 690mg | Sodium - 60mg |
Cholesterol - 0mg

13.17 Tropical Green Breakfast Smoothie

Preparation Time - 5 minutes |
Cooking Time - 0 minutes| Serves - 2

Ingredients:

- Banana cut in chunks - 1 med. Sized
- Mango cut in chunks - 1 med. Sized
- Baby spinach - 1 cup (30g)
- Plain Greek yogurt - ½ cup (120g)
- Pineapple chunks - 1 cup (165g)
- Pineapple juice or water - ¼ cup (60ml)
- Oats - ¼ cup (20g)

Procedure:

1. Place all ingredients in your blender. Process well to obtain a smooth consistency.
2. Enjoy.

Nutrition Per Serving:

Calories - 180 | Fat - 2g | Carbs - 38g |
Protein - 6g | Sugar - 20g | Fiber - 5g |
Potassium - 528mg | Sodium - 3mg |
Cholesterol - 0mg

13.18 Green Apple Smoothie

Preparation Time - 5 minutes |
Cooking Time - 0 minutes| Serves - 2

Ingredients:

- Apple cider - 1 cup (240ml)
- Banana - 1 med. Sized
- Kale, stems removed - 2 cup (60g)
- Cinnamon - a pinch
- Green apple cut into chunks - 1 cup (150g)
- Ice - 1 cup(240g)

Procedure:

1. Place all ingredients in your blender. Process well to obtain a smooth consistency.
2. Enjoy.

Nutrition Per Serving:

Calories - 120 | Fat - 1g | Carbs - 28g |
Protein - 2g | Sugar - 17g | Fiber - 4g |
Potassium - 430mg | Sodium - 31mg |
Cholesterol - 0mg

14 SNACKS RECIPES

14.1 Corn and Cayenne Pepper Spread

Preparation Time - 10 minutes |
Cooking Time - 0 minutes | Serves - 4
Ingredients:

- Cayenne pepper - ½ tsp. (1.5g)
- Boiled corn - 2 cup (300g)
- Non-fat cream cheese - 1 cup (240g)

Procedure:

1. In the bowl, combine all ingredients from the list above.
2. Carefully mix the spread.

Nutrition Per Serving:
Calories - 70 | Fat - 0.2g | Carbs - 15g |
Protein - 4g | Sugar - 3g | Fiber - 3g |
Potassium - 270mg | Sodium - 50mg |
Cholesterol - 0mg

14.2 Black Bean Bars

Preparation Time - 20 minutes |
Cooking Time - 0 minutes | Serves - 12
Ingredients:

- No-salt-added canned and drained black beans - 1 cup (240g)
- Chia seeds - ½ cup (80g)
- Coconut cream - 1 tbsp. (15ml)

Procedure:

1. In a food processor, blend the black beans until smooth, combine with chia seeds and unsweetened coconut milk.
2. Mix well to form a thick mixture.
3. Line a square baking dish with parchment paper.
4. Press the mixture into the baking dish to form a smooth and even layer.
5. Refrigerate for at least 2 hours to set.
6. Cut into bars and serve.

Nutrition Per Serving:
Calories - 90 | Fat - 2g | Carbs - 14g |
Protein - 4g | Sugar - 0.4g | Fiber - 5g |
Potassium - 220mg | Sodium - 5mg |
Cholesterol - 0mg

14.3 Roasted Red Pepper and Chickpea Hummus

Preparation Time - 10 minutes |
Cooking Time - 0 minutes | Serves - 4
Ingredients:

- No-salt-added canned chickpeas, drained and rinsed - 14 oz. (400g)
- Sesame paste - 1 tbsp. (15g)
- Roasted chopped red peppers - 2
- Lemon juice - of ½ lemon
- Chopped walnuts - 4 (30g)

Procedure:

1. In a food processor or blender, combine all the ingredients. Pulse until it reaches a smooth and creamy consistency, add a little water or lemon juice to adjust the consistency.
2. Transfer the hummus to serving bowls and enjoy it as a healthy snack or spread.

Nutrition Per Serving:
Calories - 160 | Fat - 7g | Carbs - 19g |
Protein - 6g | Sugar - 2g | Fiber - 5g |
Potassium - 260mg | Sodium - 115mg |
Cholesterol - 0mg

14.4 Lemon and Coriander Chickpea Dip

Preparation Time - 10 minutes |
Cooking Time - 0 minutes | Serves - 4

Ingredients:

- No-salt-added canned chickpeas, drained, rinsed - 14 oz. (400g)
- Lemon zest - of 1 lemon, grated
- Lemon juice - of 1 lemon
- Olive oil - 1 tbsp. (15ml)
- Pine nuts - 4 tbsp. (40g)
- Coriander, chopped - ½ cup (15g)

Procedure:

1. In a food processor or blender, combine the lemon juice, olive oil, lemon zest, chopped coriander, and chickpeas.
2. Pulse the mixture until it becomes smooth and creamy.
3. Transfer the dip to serving bowls and top with sprinkles of pine nuts before serving.
4. Serve with olive oil and coriander topping and enjoy with whole-grain crackers.

Nutrition Per Serving:

Calories - 160 | Fat - 7g | Carbs - 19g |
Protein - 6g | Sugar - 0.4g | Fiber - 5g |
Potassium - 310mg | Sodium - 120mg |
Cholesterol - 0mg

14.5 Red Pepper and Mozzarella Muffins

Preparation Time - 15 minutes |
Cooking Time - 20 minutes | Serves - 12

Ingredients:

- Flour (whole wheat) - 1¾ cup (220g)
- Coconut sugar - 2 tbsp. (24g)
- Baking powder - 2 tsp. (8g)
- Black pepper - a pinch
- Egg - 1
- Unsweetened almond milk - ¾ cup (180ml)
- Red pepper, roasted and chopped - ⅔ cup (100g)
- Low-fat shredded mozzarella - ½ cup (60g)

Procedure:

1. Preheat oven to 375°F (190°C). Line/grease muffin tray. Whisk coconut sugar, whole wheat flour, baking powder, and pepper.
2. In a separate bowl, beat egg, add almond milk, red pepper, mozzarella. Combine wet and dry ingredients, avoiding over-mixing.
3. Divide batter into 12 muffin cups. Bake for 18-20 minutes. Cool for 5 minutes in tray, then transfer to a wire rack. Enjoy these red pepper mozzarella muffins as a snack or breakfast.

Nutrition Per Serving:

Calories - 120 | Fat - 3g | Carbs - 20g |
Protein - 5g | Sugar - 2g | Fiber - 3g |
Potassium - 160mg | Sodium - 110mg |
Cholesterol - 20mg

14.6 Nuts And Seed Trail Mix

Preparation Time - 10 minutes |
Cooking Time - 0 minutes| Serves - 6

Ingredients:

- Pecans - 1 cup (120g)
- Hazelnuts - 1 cup (120g)
- Almonds - 1 cup (120g)
- Shredded coconut - ¼ cup (20g)
- Walnuts - 1 cup (120g)
- Dried papaya pieces - ½ cup (75g)
- Dates, dried, pitted and chopped - ½ cup (85g)
- Sunflower seeds - ½ cup (70g)
- Pumpkin seeds - ½ cup (65g)
- Raisins - 1 cup (150g)

Procedure:

1. In a large bowl, combine the pecans, hazelnuts, almonds, walnuts, shredded coconut, dried papaya pieces, chopped dates, sunflower seeds, pumpkin seeds, and raisins. Toss everything together until well mixed.
2. Serve and enjoy this delicious and nutritious nut and seed trail mix as a healthy snack.

Nutrition Per Serving:

Calories - 280 | Fat - 20g | Carbs - 24g | Protein - 7g | Sugar - 12g | Fiber - 6g | Potassium - 340mg | Sodium - 2mg | Cholesterol - 0mg

14.7 Baked Tortilla Chips with Chili

Preparation Time - 10 minutes |
Cooking Time - 20 minutes| Serves - 6

Ingredients:

- Whole wheat tortillas, each cut into 6 wedges - 12
- Olive oil - 2 tbsp. (30ml)
- Chili powder - 1 tbsp. (8g)
- Cayenne pepper - a pinch

Procedure:

1. Preheat your oven to 350°F (180°C). Line a baking sheet with aluminum foil.
2. In a large bowl, toss the tortilla wedges with olive oil, chili powder, and a pinch of cayenne pepper until they are evenly coated.
3. Arrange the seasoned tortilla wedges in a single layer on the prepared baking sheet.
4. Bake in the preheated oven for about 15-20 minutes or until they are crispy and golden brown.
5. Remove from the oven and let them cool slightly before serving.
6. Enjoy these baked tortilla chips with chili dip as a flavorful and healthier alternative to store-bought chips.

Nutrition Per Serving:

Calories - 90 | Fat - 2g | Carbs - 14g | Protein - 4g | Sugar - 0.4g | Fiber - 5g | Potassium - 220mg | Sodium - 70mg | Cholesterol - 0mg

14.8 Baked Kale Chips

Preparation Time - 10 minutes |
Cooking Time - 15 minutes| Serves - 8

Ingredients:

- Kale leaves - 1 bunch (about 250g)
- Olive oil - 1 tbsp. (15ml)
- Smoked paprika - 1 tsp. (2g)
- Black pepper - a pinch

Procedure:

1. Preheat your oven to 350°F (180°C). Line a baking sheet with parchment paper.
2. Wash and thoroughly dry the kale leaves. Remove the tough stems and tear the leaves into bite-sized pieces.
3. In a large bowl, toss the kale pieces with olive oil, smoked paprika, and a pinch of black pepper until they are evenly coated.
4. Arrange the seasoned kale pieces in a single layer on the prepared baking sheet.
5. Bake in the preheated oven for about 12-15 minutes or until the kale leaves are crispy but not burnt.
6. Remove from the oven and let them cool slightly before serving.

Nutrition Per Serving: Calories - 30 | Fat - 1g | Carbs - 4g | Protein - 2g | Sugar - 0.5g | Fiber - 2g | Potassium - 250mg | Sodium - 30mg | Cholesterol - 0mg

14.9 Hearty Walnut Butter Bites

Preparation Time - 10 minutes |
Cooking Time - 0 minutes| Serves - 4

Ingredients:

- Walnut halves - 8 (about 30g)
- Almond butter - 2 tbsp. (30g)

Procedure:

1. Finely chop the walnuts, mix in melted butter and refrigerate.
2. When the butter is hardened scoop out and form small bite sized balls. Let set in the refrigerator for half an hour and enjoy!

Nutrition Per Serving: Calories - 120 | Fat - 10g | Carbs - 4g | Protein - 3g | Sugar - 1g | Fiber - 2g | Potassium - 80mg | Sodium - 0mg | Cholesterol - 0mg

14.10 Spiced Walnuts

Preparation Time - 5 minutes |
Cooking Time - 15 minutes | Serves - 4

Ingredients:

- Walnuts - 2 cup (240g)
- Red vinegar - 3 tbsp. (45ml)
- Olive oil - 1 tbsp. (15ml)
- Cayenne pepper - a pinch

Procedure:

1. Preheat your oven to 350°F (175°C).
2. In a mixing bowl, toss the walnuts with red wine vinegar, olive oil, and a pinch of cayenne pepper until the walnuts are evenly coated with the spices.
3. Spread the spiced walnuts in a single layer on a lined baking tray. Roast the walnuts in the preheated oven for about 15 minutes, stirring occasionally to ensure even roasting and to prevent burning.
4. Once the walnuts are fragrant and lightly toasted, remove them from the oven and let them cool completely before serving.

Nutrition Per Serving:

Calories - 260 | Fat - 25g | Carbs - 6g | Protein - 6g | Sugar - 1g | Fiber - 3g | Potassium - 170mg | Sodium - 5mg | Cholesterol - 0mg

14.11 Radish Chips

Preparation Time - 10 minutes |
Cooking Time - 20 minutes | Serves - 4

Ingredients:

- Radishes, thinly sliced - 1 pound (454g)
- Olive oil - 2 tbsp. (30ml)

Procedure:

1. Preheat your oven to 365°F (185°C).
2. Mix radish slices with olive oil and transfer them to a baking tray.
3. Bake the chips for approx. 20 minutes at 365°F. Toss them to avoid burning.
4. Once the radish chips are crispy and lightly browned, remove them from the oven and serve fresh.

Nutrition Per Serving: Calories - 90 | Fat - 2g Carbs - 14g | Protein - 4g | Sugar - 0.4g | Fiber - 5g | Potassium - 220mg | Sodium - 40mg | Cholesterol - 0mg

14.12 Aromatic Avocado Fries

Preparation Time - 5 minutes |
Cooking Time - 10 minutes| Serves - 4

Ingredients:

- Avocados, peeled and pitted, cut into wedges - 2 med. sized
- Avocado oil - 1 tbsp. (15ml)
- Ground cardamom - 1 tsp. (5g)

Procedure:

1. Preheat your oven to 375°F (190°C).
2. In a bowl, toss the avocado wedges with oil and cardamom until they are coated.
3. Line a baking tray and arrange the avocado wedges on the tray in a single layer.
4. Bake the avocado fries in the oven for 10 minutes, flipping them over to ensure even cooking. Once the avocado fries are crispy and golden, remove them and serve fresh.

Nutrition Per Serving:
Calories - 90 | Fat - 7g | Carbs - 6g | Protein - 1g | Sugar - 0.4g | Fiber - 4g | Potassium - 212mg | Sodium - 1mg | Cholesterol - 0mg

14.13 Carrot Chips

Preparation Time - 10 minutes |
Cooking Time - 25 minutes | Serves - 4

Ingredients:

- Carrots, thinly sliced - 4 med. sized
- Avocado oil - 2 tbsp. (30ml)
- Chili flakes - 1 tsp. (2g)
- Turmeric powder - ½ tsp.(1g)

Procedure:

1. Preheat your oven to 400°F (200°C).
2. In a bowl, mix the thinly sliced carrots with oil, chili flakes, and turmeric powder until the carrots are well coated.
3. Place the carrot slices on a lined baking sheet in a single layer. Bake the carrot chips in the oven for approximately 25 minutes, toss them to ensure even cooking.
4. Once the carrot chips are crispy and lightly golden, remove them and serve fresh.

Nutrition Per Serving:
Calories - 90 | Fat - 6g | Carbs - 9g | Protein - 1g | Sugar - 4g | Fiber - 3g | Potassium - 239mg | Sodium - 11mg | Cholesterol - 0mg

14.14 Minty Tapenade

Preparation Time - 10 minutes |
Cooking Time - 0 minutes | Serves - 4

Ingredients:

- Black olives, pitted and chopped - 1 cup (160g)
- Mint, chopped - ½ cup (30g)
- Avocado oil - 2 tbsp. (30ml)
- Coconut cream - ½ cup (120ml)

Procedure:

1. In a blender or food processor, combine the chopped black olives, chopped mint, avocado oil, and coconut cream.
2. Blend the ingredients until you achieve a smooth and creamy consistency.
3. Transfer the Tapenade to a serving bowl.

Nutrition Per Serving: Calories - 90 | Fat - 6g | Carbs - 6g | Protein - 1g | Sugar - 0.2g | Fiber - 2g | Potassium - 105mg | Sodium - 135mg | Cholesterol - 0mg

14.15 Nutritious Snack Bowls

Preparation Time - 5 minutes |
Cooking Time - 0 minutes| Serves - 4
Ingredients:

- Sunflower seeds - 1 cup(120g)
- Chia seeds - 1 cup (160g)
- Water - 1 cup (240ml)
- Apples, chord cut into wedges - 2 med. sized
- Ground cardamom - ¼ tsp. (0.5g)

Procedure:

1. In a bowl, mix 1 cup of water with chia seeds and ground cardamom. Stir gently and let the mixture sit for 20 minutes to form a chia gel.
2. In another bowl, combine the soaked chia seeds, sunflower seeds, and apple wedges, gently mix everything together, and serve.

Nutrition Per Serving:

Calories - 180 | Fat - 9g | Carbs - 21g | Protein - 6g | Sugar - 9g | Fiber - 10g | Potassium - 340mg | Sodium - 5mg | Cholesterol - 0mg

14.16 Potato Chips

Preparation Time - 15 minutes |
Cooking Time - 20 minutes| Serves - 4
Ingredients:

- Gold potatoes, peeled, thinly sliced - 4
- Garlic powder - ¼ tsp.
- Olive oil - 2 tbsp.
- Sweet paprika - 1 tsp.

Procedure:

1. Preheat the oven to 390°F (200°C) and line a baking sheet.
2. In a bowl, toss the thinly sliced potatoes with olive oil, garlic powder, and sweet paprika until they are evenly coated.
3. Arrange the potato slices in a single layer on the prepared baking sheet, Bake the chips until they are golden brown and crispy, flipping them over to cook the other side.

Nutrition Per Serving: Calories - 180 | Fat - 7g | Carbs - 29g | Protein - 3g | Sugar - 2g | Fiber - 5g | Potassium - 570mg | Sodium - 20mg | Cholesterol - 0mg

14.17 Hot Walnuts

Preparation Time - 5 minutes |
Cooking Time - 15 minutes| Serves - 8
Ingredients:

- Smoked paprika - ½ tsp. (1g)
- Chili powder - ½ tsp. (1g)
- Garlic powder - ½ tsp. (1g)
- Avocado oil - 1 tbsp. (15ml)
- Walnuts - 14 oz. (400g)

Procedure:

1. Preheat your oven to 355°F (180°C).
2. In a bowl, add the walnuts and evenly coat with the spices and oil.
3. Spread the coated walnuts on a baking tray in a single layer.
4. Bake the walnuts in the oven for about 15 minutes, stirring them occasionally to ensure even cooking.
5. Serve fresh, once they are nicely toasted

Nutrition Per Serving:

Calories - 180 | Fat - 17g | Carbs - 5g | Protein - 4g | Sugar - 1g | Fiber - 3g | Potassium - 120mg | Sodium - 60mg | Cholesterol - 0mg

14.18 Cranberry Crackers

Preparation Time - 15 minutes |
Cooking Time - 50 minutes | Freezing Time - 2 hours| Serves - 4
Ingredients:

- Vanilla extract - ¼ tsp. (1.25ml)
- Rolled oats - 2 tbsp. (16g)
- Shredded coconut - 2 tbsp. (16g)
- Cranberries - 1 cup (100g)

Procedure:

1. Preheat oven to 350°F (180°C), blend the ingredients until a sticky dough forms. Press into a lined dish. Bake at 250°F (120°C) for 25 minutes.
2. Cool, wrap in cling film, freeze for 2 hours. Partially thaw (15 minutes).
3. Slice into crackers, place on baking pans. Bake for 15-20 minutes until golden, tossing midway, cool for crispness.

Nutrition Per Serving:

Calories - 180 | Fat - 7g | Carbs - 30g | Protein - 3g | Sugar - 13g | Fiber - 4g | Potassium - 130mg | Sodium - 10mg | Cholesterol - 0mg

15 SAUCES AND DRESSING RECIPES

15.1 Salsa Verde

Preparation Time - 10 minutes |
Cooking Time - 0 minutes| Serves - 5
Ingredients:

- Cilantro, fresh finely chopped - 4 tbsp. (15g)
- Parsley, fresh finely chopped - ¼ cup (15g)
- Garlic cloves, grated - 2
- Lemon juice - 2 tsp. (10ml)
- Olive oil - ¾ cup (180ml)
- Capers - 2 tbsp. (28g)
- Black pepper - ½ tsp. (2.5g)

Procedure:

1. In a bowl, combine the finely chopped cilantro, parsley, grated garlic cloves, lemon juice, olive oil, capers, and black pepper. Mix well using a spoon or an immersion blender until the desired consistency is achieved.
2. Serve the Salsa Verde over burgers, sandwiches, salads, and more. You can refrigerate it for up to 5 days, or freeze it for longer storage.

Nutrition Per Serving:

Calories - 120 | Fat - 13g | Carbs - 1g |
Protein - 1g | Sugar - 0.3g | Fiber - 0.3g |
Potassium - 35mg | Sodium - 50mg |
Cholesterol - 0mg

15.2 Caramel Sauce

Preparation Time - 5 minutes |
Cooking Time - 20 minutes| Serves - 8
Ingredients:

- Raw cashews - ½ cup (60g)
- Coconut cream, melted - ½ cup (120ml)
- Liquid stevia - 10 drops
- Vegan butter - 2 tbsp. (30ml)
- Vanilla extract - 3 tsp. (15ml)

Procedure:

1. Preheat your oven to 325°F (165°C).
2. Spread the raw cashews on a greased baking tray and toast them in the preheated oven for about 10 minutes or until they are crunchy and lightly golden. Let the toasted cashews cool slightly.
3. In a food processor, pulse the toasted cashews until they reach a slightly lumpy consistency.
4. Add the melted coconut cream, liquid stevia, vegan butter, and vanilla extract to the food processor. Blend well until you achieve a smooth and creamy consistency. Be careful not to over-blend to prevent the coconut cream from separating.
5. If not using immediately, store the caramel sauce in an airtight container in the refrigerator.
6. To reheat the caramel sauce and make it more pour able, gently warm it in a saucepan over low heat. This delicious caramel sauce can be served with your favorite keto vegan treats, such as ice cream or desserts.

Nutrition Per Serving:

Calories - 80 | Fat - 5g | Carbs - 8g |
Protein - 1g | Sugar - 2g | Fiber - 1g |
Potassium - 80mg | Sodium - 5mg |
Cholesterol - 0mg

15.3 Authentic Greek Tzatziki Sauce

Preparation Time - 15 minutes |
Cooking Time – 0| Serves - 6

Ingredients:

- Plain Greek yogurt - 1 cup (240g)
- Persian cucumbers, grated - 2 med. sized
- Extra-virgin olive oil - 1 tbsp. (15ml)
- Dill, chopped fresh - 2 tbsp. (30g)
- Mint, freshly chopped - 2 tbsp. (30g)
- Garlic clove, minced - 1
- Lemon juice - 2 tbsp. (30ml)
- Kosher salt - ½ tsp. (2.5g)

Procedure:

1. Squeeze out any excess moisture in cucumbers, using your hands.
2. In a medium bowl, combine all the ingredients. Mix well until evenly incorporated.
3. Refrigerate the Tzatziki sauce for at least 30 minutes before serving to allow the flavors to meld together.
4. Serve as a refreshing and tangy sauce with your favorite Greek dishes, grilled meats, or as a dip with fresh vegetables.

Nutrition Per Serving:

Calories - 25 | Fat - 1g | Carbs - 2g |
Protein - 1g | Sugar - 1g | Fiber - 0.2g |
Potassium - 75mg | Sodium - 98mg |
Cholesterol - 1mg

15.4 Beef Taco Filling

Preparation Time - 10 minutes |
Cooking Time - 20 minutes| Serves - 4

Ingredients:

- Ground extra lean sirloin, 95% lean - 1 pound (454g)
- Medium taco sauce - ½ cup (120g)
- Green peppers, finely chopped (fresh or frozen) - 1 cup (150g)
- Onions, diced (fresh or frozen) - 1 cup (150g)

Procedure:

1. In a nonstick skillet, add the ground beef and cook over medium-high heat for about 3 minutes. Reduce the heat to medium and add the onions and peppers. Continue to cook for 5 minutes or until the beef is thoroughly browned.
2. Add the taco sauce to the skillet, reduce the heat to low, and let it simmer for 10 minutes.
3. Serve the beef taco filling in your favorite taco shells or tortillas along with your preferred toppings.

Nutrition Per Serving:

Calories - 180 | Fat - 7g | Carbs 6g |
Protein - 25g | Sugar - 3g | Fiber - 2g |
Potassium - 530mg | Sodium - 220mg |
Cholesterol - 60mg

15.5 Creamy Avocado Alfredo Sauce

Preparation Time - 10 minutes |
Cooking Time - 2 minutes| Serves - 4

Ingredients:

- Ripe avocado, peeled and pitted - 1 med. Sized
- Olive oil - 1 tbsp.(15ml)
- Dried basil - 1 tbsp. (6g)
- Garlic clove - 1
- Lemon juice - 1 tbsp. (15ml)
- Salt - ⅛ tsp. (0.6g)

Procedure:

1. In a food processor, combine the peeled and pitted avocado, olive oil, dried basil, clove of garlic, lemon juice, and salt. Blend until you get a smooth and creamy sauce.
2. Pour the avocado Alfredo sauce over vegetable noodles or your preferred dish and enjoy the creamy goodness!

Nutrition Per Serving:

Calories - 180 | Fat - 14g | Carbs - 10g |
Protein - 2g | Sugar - 1g | Fiber - 5g |
Potassium - 440mg | Sodium - 30mg |
Cholesterol - 0mg

15.6 Vegan Ranch Dressing

Preparation Time - 10 minutes |
Cooking Time - 0 minutes | Serves - 6

Ingredients:

- Vegan mayo - 1 cup (240ml)
- Coconut milk - 1½ cup (360ml)
- Scallions - 2
- Peeled garlic cloves - 2
- Fresh dill - 1 cup (240g)
- Garlic powder - 1 tsp. (2g)
- Pepper - ¼ tsp. (0.5g)

Procedure:

1. In a food processor, add the chopped scallions, fresh dill, and peeled garlic cloves. Pulse until finely chopped.
2. Add the vegan mayo, unsweetened coconut milk,garlic powder, and black pepper to the food processor. Blend until the mixture is smooth and creamy.
3. Transfer the dressing to an airtight container and store it in the refrigerator.

Nutrition Per Serving:

Calories - 90 | Fat - 7g | Carbs - 6g |
Protein - 1g | Sugar - 1g | Fiber - 0.3g |
Potassium - 43mg | Sodium - 32mg |
Cholesterol - 0mg

15.7 Easy Quick Tangy Barbecue Sauce

Preparation Time - 5 minutes |
Cooking Time - 1 min | Serves - 12

Ingredients:

- No-salt tomato paste - 1 (8 oz.) can (227g)
- Apple cider vinegar - 1½ tbsp. (10.5ml)
- Dijon mustard - 2 tbsp. (30g)
- Onion powder - 1 tsp. (2g)
- Molasses - 2 tsp. (10ml)
- Soy sauce (low-sodium) - 1 tbsp. (15ml)
- Garlic powder - 1 tsp. (2g)

Procedure:

1. In a medium bowl, combine the garlic powder, tomato paste, soy sauce, apple cider vinegar, Dijon mustard, molasses, and onion powder. Mix well until all ingredients are thoroughly incorporated.
2. Transfer the sauce to an airtight container and refrigerate. The barbecue sauce can be stored in the refrigerator for up to one week.

Nutrition Per Serving:

Calories - 15 | Fat - 0.1g | Carbs - 3g | Protein - 1g | Sugar - 2g | Fiber - 1g | Potassium - 64mg | Sodium - 34mg | Cholesterol - 0mg

15.8 Fresh Tomato Basil Sauce

Preparation Time - 5 minutes |
Cooking Time - 20 minutes | Serves - 6

Ingredients:

- Olive oil - 2 tbsp. (30ml)
- Tomatoes - crushed, or chopped - 4 (15 oz.) (425g) cans
- Garlic cloves, finely chopped - 3
- Dried basil - 1 tbsp. (6g)
- Salt - ¼ tsp. (1.2g)
- Freshly ground black pepper - ¼ tsp. (0.6g)

Procedure:

1. In a large saucepan, heat the olive oil over medium heat. Add the finely chopped garlic and sauté for about 1 minute, being careful not to burn it. Stir in the dried basil and the canned tomatoes. Season with salt and pepper. Cook the sauce uncovered over medium heat for about 20 minutes, stirring occasionally.
2. Serve the tomato basil sauce over pasta, grains, beans, or vegetables, adding a healthy and flavorful touch to your DASH diet meals.

Nutrition Per Serving:

Calories - 50 | Fat - 2g | Carbs - 8g | Protein - 1g | Sugar - 5g | Fiber - 2g | Potassium - 182mg | Sodium - 15mg | Cholesterol - 0mg

15.9 Greek Yogurt Dressing with Basil

Preparation Time - 5 minutes |
Cooking Time - 10 minutes| Serves - 2
Ingredients:

- Fresh basil, chopped - ¼ cup (10g)
- Sage, chopped - ¼ cup (10g)
- Non-fat (0%) plain Greek yogurt - 1 cup (240ml)
- Fresh coriander, chopped - ½ cup (20g)
- Onion, minced - 1 small sized
- Garlic cloves, minced - 2
- Extra-virgin olive oil - 2 tbsp. (30ml)
- Juice from 1 orange - 2 tbsp. (30ml)
- Maple syrup - ½ tsp. (2.5ml)
- Salt - ⅛ tsp. (0.6g)
- Ground black pepper - ⅛ tsp. (0.6g)

Procedure:

1. In a food processor, combine the basil, sage, and coriander (cilantro). Pulse a few times until they are slightly ground. Scrape down the sides of the food processor.
2. Add the minced onion, minced garlic, Greek yogurt, olive oil, salt, orange juice, ¼ cup of water, maple syrup, and black pepper to the food processor. Puree until the mixture is smooth and all the ingredients are fully incorporated.
3. Enjoy the Greek yogurt dressing with basil immediately or refrigerate it in an airtight container for a maximum of 1 week.

Nutrition Per Serving:

Calories - 30 | Fat - 2g | Carbs - 2g |
Protein - 2g | Sugar - 1g | Fiber - 1g |
Potassium - 64mg | Sodium - 29mg |
Cholesterol - 0mg

15.10 Meaty Spaghetti Sauce

Preparation Time - 15 minutes |
Cooking Time - 30 minutes| Serves - 6
Ingredients:

- Ground 95% lean beef, extra-lean - 1 pound (454g)
- No salt added tomato sauce - 1 (15 oz.) can (425g)
- Tomatoes, no salt added - 1 (14½ oz.) can (411g)
- Garlic cloves, minced - 2
- Chopped onions (fresh or frozen) - ½ cup (80g)
- Italian seasoning - 1 tsp.(2g)
- Dried basil - 1 tsp. (2g)
- Olive oil - spray for skillet

Procedure:

1. In a nonstick skillet set over medium-high heat, lightly spray with olive oil and add ground beef. Cook for about 3 minutes until it starts to brown. Reduce the heat to medium and add in garlic and onions. Continue cooking for an additional 5 minutes, or until the beef is well browned and onions are tender.
2. Add the diced tomatoes and tomato sauce to the skillet. Simmer for 10 - 15 minutes, allowing the flavors to meld together. Sprinkle the Italian seasoning and dried basil during the last few minutes of cooking.
3. Serve the meaty spaghetti sauce over your favorite wholegrain pasta or vegetable noodles.

Nutrition Per Serving:

Calories - 180 | Fat - 6g | Carbs - 13g |
Protein - 19g | Sugar - 6g | Fiber - 3g |
Potassium - 416mg | Sodium - 35mg |
Cholesterol - 51mg

15.11 Creamy Avocado Cilantro Lime Dressing

Preparation Time - 5 minutes |
Cooking Time - 0 minutes | Serves - 4
Ingredients:
- Diced avocado - 1 med. Sized
- Water - ½ cup (120g)
- Fresh cilantro leaves - ¼ cup (15g)
- Fresh lime or lemon juice - ¼ cup (60ml)
- Ground cumin - ½ tsp. (1g)
- Salt - a pinch (adjust to taste)

Procedure:
1. Using a blender, add all the ingredients (high-speed blenders work best for this), and pulse until well combined. Add more seasoning if needed. It is best served within 1 day.

Nutrition Per Serving:
Calories - 45 | Fat - 3g | Carbs - 6g |
Protein - 1g | Sugar - 1g | Fiber - 2g |
Potassium - 100mg | Sodium - 63mg |
Cholesterol - 0mg

15.12 Maple Dijon Dressing

Preparation Time - 5 minutes |
Cooking Time - 0 minutes | Serves - 8
Ingredients:
- Apple cider vinegar - ¼ cup (60ml)
- Dijon mustard - 2 tsp. (30g)
- Maple syrup - 2 tbsp. (30ml)
- Low-sodium vegetable broth - 2 tbsp. (30ml)
- Black pepper - ¼ tsp. (0.5g)

Procedure:
1. Using a resealable container, mix the apple cider vinegar, maple syrup, vegetable broth, Dijon mustard, and black pepper until well incorporated.
2. The dressing can be refrigerated for a maximum of 5 days.

Nutrition Per Serving:
Calories - 45 | Fat - 0.3g | Carbs - 11g |
Protein - 0.4g | Sugar - 9g | Fiber - 0.3g |
Potassium - 37mg | Sodium - 34mg |
Cholesterol - 0mg

15.13 Tahini Lemon Dressing

Preparation Time - 5 minutes |
Cooking Time - 0 | Serves - 2
Ingredients:
- Pure maple syrup - 1 tsp. (5g)
- Tahini - ¼ cup (60g)
- Warm water - 3 tbsp. (45ml)
- Cumin (ground) - ¼ tsp.
- Kosher salt - ¼ tsp.
- Lemon juice - 3 tbsp.
- Cayenne pepper - ⅛ tsp.

Procedure:
1. In a bowl, add warm water, ground cumin, kosher salt, cayenne pepper, tahini, lemon juice, and pure maple syrup. Mix well until the mixture becomes smooth.
2. Refrigerate the dressing until it is ready to serve.
3. Store any leftovers in an airtight container and place it in the refrigerator for a maximum of 5 days.

Nutrition Per Serving: Calories - 90 | Fat - 7g
Carbs - 6g | Protein - 3g | Sugar - 2g |
Fiber - 1g | Potassium - 65mg |
Sodium - 130mg | Cholesterol - 0mg

15.14 Tahini Yogurt Dressing

Preparation Time - 5 minutes |
Cooking Time – 0 | Serves - 4
Ingredients:
- Plain Greek yogurt - ½ cup (120g)
- Tahini - ⅓ cup (80g)
- Freshly squeezed orange juice - ¼ cup (60ml)
- Kosher salt - ½ tsp. (2.5g)

Procedure:
1. In a mixing bowl, combine the tahini, freshly squeezed orange juice, and kosher salt. Mix well until smooth. Add more orange juice if needed to achieve a smoother consistency. Refrigerate the dressing until it is ready to serve.

Nutrition Per Serving:
Calories - 90 | Fat - 7g | Carbs - 5g |
Protein - 3g | Sugar - 3g | Fiber - 1g |
Potassium - 65mg | Sodium - 60mg |
Cholesterol - 0mg

16 10 WEEKS MEAL PLAN

16.1 Week 1

Monday
Breakfast - 3.1 Millet Cream (p.11, Cal 989)
Snack - 4.1 Shrimp and Veggie Salad (p.15, Cal 390)
Lunch - 8.1 Vegetarian Black Bean Pasta (p.40, Cal 255)
Snack - 9.15 Honey Sage Carrots (p.50, Cal 217)
Dinner - 6.1 Cilantro Halibut (p.23, Cal 365)
Nutrition Per Day:
Calories - 2216 | Fat - 34g | Carbs - 132g | Protein - 112g | Sugar - 222mg | Fiber - 31g | Potassium - 3982mg | Sodium - 1187mg | Cholesterol - 404mg

Tuesday
Breakfast - 3.2 The Amazing Feta Fish (p.11, Cal 303)
Snack - 4.2 Spinach and Salmon Salad (p.15, Cal 155)
Lunch - 8.2 Lentil Medley (p.40, Cal 225)
Snack - 9.14 Italians Style Mushroom Mix (p.50, Cal 96)
Dinner - 6.2 Shallot and Salmon Mix (p.23, Cal 369)
Nutrition Per Day:
Calories - 1148 | Fat - 44g | Carbs - 85g | Protein - 76g | Sugar - 42.9mg | Fiber - 39g | Potassium - 5255mg | Sodium - 1497mg | Cholesterol - 400mg

Wednesday
Breakfast - 3.3 Sausage Casserole (p.12, Cal 74)
Snack - 4.3 Corn Salad (p.16, Cal 159)
Lunch - 8.3 Zucchini with Corn (p.41, Cal 202)
Snack - 9.13 Parsley Red Potatoes (p.49, Cal 256)
Dinner - 6.3 Lime and Shrimp Mix (p.23, Cal 141)
Nutrition Per Day:
Calories - 832 | Fat - 23g | Carbs - 106g | Protein - 63.5g | Sugar - 12.7mg | Fiber - 36g | Potassium - 1737mg | Sodium - 1654mg | Cholesterol - 383mg

Thursday
Breakfast - 3.4 Apples and Raisins Bowls (p.12, Cal 266)
Snack - 4.4 Watercress Salad (p.16, Cal 264)
Lunch - 8.4 Couscous with Beans & Vegetables (p.41, Cal 330)
Snack - 9.12 Parsley Fennel (p.49, Cal 47)
Dinner - 6.4 Tuna and Pineapple Kabob (p.29, Cal 135)
Nutrition Per Day:
Calories - 1042 | Fat - 24.5g | Carbs - 128g | Protein - 51.4g | Sugar - 59.4mg | Fiber - 55g | Potassium - 6691mg | Sodium - 828mg | Cholesterol - 505mg

Friday
Breakfast - 3.5 Dill Omelet (p.12, Cal 71)
Snack - 4.5 Tuna Salad (p.16, Cal 173)
Lunch - 8.5 Roasted Kabocha with Wild Rice (p.42, Cal 250)
Snack - 9.11 Carrot Sticks with Onion and Sour Cream (p.48, Cal 60)
Dinner - 6.5 Coconut Cod (p.24, Cal 191)
Nutrition Per Day:
Calories - 745 | Fat - 39.3g | Carbs - 48.2g | Protein - 57.2g | Sugar - 18mg | Fiber - 26.9g | Potassium - 3131mg | Sodium - 467mg | Cholesterol - 306mg

Saturday
Breakfast - 3.6 Cheese Hash Browns (p.12, Cal 212)
Snack - 4.6 Watermelon Salad (p.16, Cal 218)
Lunch - 8.6 Acorn Squash & Coconut Creamed Greens Casserole (p.42, Cal 248)
Snack - 9.10 Pomegranate & Ricotta Bruschetta (p.48, Cal 69)
Dinner - 6.6 Ginger Sea Bass (p.24, Cal 191)
Nutrition Per Day:
Calories - 938 | Fat - 51.2g | Carbs - 76g | Protein - 54g | Sugar - 42mg | Fiber - 33.5g | Potassium - 2522mg | Sodium - 1324mg | Cholesterol - 299mg

Sunday

Breakfast - 3.7 Tomato and Spinach Eggs (p.13, Cal 202)
Snack - 4.7 Orange Celery Salad (p.17, Cal 65)
Lunch - 8.7 Warm Spiced Cabbage Bake (p.43, Cal 131)
Snack - 9.9 Fresh Fruit Kebabs (p.48, Cal 27)
Dinner - 6.7 Baked Cod (p.25, Cal 150)
Nutrition Per Day:
Calories - 575 | Fat - 38g | Carbs - 37g | Protein - 71.5g | Sugar - 36mg | Fiber - 45g | Potassium - 3130mg | Sodium - 589mg | Cholesterol - 392mg

16.2 Week 2

Monday

Breakfast - 3.8 Scallions and Sesame (p.13, Cal 101)
Snack - 4.8 Lettuce & Cucumber Salad (p.17, Cal 88)
Lunch - 8.8 Curried Cauliflower with Chickpeas (p.43, Cal 224)
Snack - 9.8 Chinese-Style Asparagus (p.47, Cal 260)
Dinner - 6.8 Five-Spices Sole (p.25, Cal 180)
Nutrition Per Day:
Calories - 853 | Fat - 28g | Carbs - 71g | Protein - 69g | Sugar - 10mg | Fiber - 44g | Potassium - 4389mg | Sodium - 524mg | Cholesterol - 279mg

Tuesday

Breakfast - 3.9 Omelet with Peppers (p.13, Cal 102)
Snack - 4.9 Seafood Arugula Salad (p.17, Cal 155)
Lunch - 7.1 Roasted Brussels Sprouts (p.28, Cal 134)
Snack - 9.7 Mashed Cauliflower with Garlic (p.47, Cal 67)
Dinner - 6.9 Parsley Shrimp (p.25, Cal 120)
Nutrition Per Day:
Calories - 578 | Fat - 33g | Carbs - 26g | Protein - 50g | Sugar - 2g | Fiber - 31g | Potassium - 1458mg | Sodium - 995mg | Cholesterol - 664mg

Wednesday

Breakfast - 3.10 Artichoke Eggs (p.13, Cal 176)
Snacks - 5.1 Lemon & Garlic Soup (p.18, Cal 101)
Lunch - 7.2 Chunky Black-Bean Dip (p.28, Cal 70)
Snacks - 9.6 Spiced Broccoli Florets (p.46, Cal 119)
Dinner - 6.10 Tender Salmon with Chives (p.26, Cal 250)
Nutrition Per Day:
Calories - 716 | Fat - 39g | Carbs - 32.6g | Protein - 54g | Sugar - 28mg | Fiber - 49g | Potassium - 3323mg | Sodium - 990mg | Cholesterol - 344mg

Thursday

Breakfast - 3.11 Beam Casserole (p.14, Cal 143)
Snacks - 5.2 Healthy Cucumber Soup (p.18, Cal 371)
Lunch - 7.3 Greek Flat bread with Spinach, Tomatoes & Feta (p.29, Cal 410)
Snacks - 9.5 Chive & Garlic Mash (p.46, Cal 292)
Dinner - 6.11 Fennel and Salmon (p.26, Cal 250)
Nutrition Per Day:
Calories - 1466 | Fat - 85g | Carbs - 119g | Protein - 65g | Sugar - 11mg | Fiber - 25g | Potassium - 3155mg | Sodium - 1510mg | Cholesterol - 195mg

Friday

Breakfast - 3.12 Strawberry Sandwich (p.14, Cal 84)

Snacks - 5.3 Amazing Pumpkin Soup (p.19, Cal 61)

Lunch - 7.4 Black-Bean and Vegetable Burrito (p.29, Cal 311)

Snacks - 9.4 Peach And Carrots (p.45, Cal 139)

Dinner - 6.12 Cod and Asparagus (p.27, Cal 190)

Nutrition Per Day:

Calories - 785 | Fat - 25g | Carbs - 118g | Protein - 61g | Sugar - 15mg | Fiber - 35g | Potassium - 1573mg | Sodium - 885mg | Cholesterol - 66mg

Saturday

Breakfast - 13.1 Blueberry-Vanilla Yogurt (p.69, Cal 186)

Snacks - 5.4 Coconut Avocado Soup (p.19, Cal 250)

Lunch - 7.5 Red Beans and Rice (p.30, Cal 232)

Snacks - 9.3 Cumin Brussels Sprouts (p.45, Cal 56)

Dinner - 10.1 Turkey with Spring Onions (p.51, Cal 179)

Nutrition Per Day:

Calories - 903 | Fat - 40g | Carbs - 102g | Protein - 55g | Sugar - 31g | Fiber - 43.71g | Potassium - 2332mg | Sodium - 455mg | Cholesterol - 65mg

Sunday

Breakfast - 13.2 Peaches And Greens (p.69, Cal 105)

Snacks - 5.5 Pumpkin & Garlic Soup (p.20, Cal 234)

Lunch - 7.6 Veggies Pita Rolls (p.30, Cal 334)

Snacks - 9.2 Sour Cream Green Beans (p.44, Cal 360)

Dinner - 10.2 Chicken with Tomatoes and Celery Stalk (p.51, Cal 265)

Nutrition Per Day:

Calories - 1298 | Fat - 52.7g | Carbs - 152.5g | Protein - 70g | Sugar - 38g | Fiber - 22g | Potassium - 4036mg | Sodium - 1107mg | Cholesterol - 117mg

16.3 Week 3

Monday

Breakfast - 13.3 Banana Breakfast Smoothie (p.69, Cal 82)

Snacks - 5.6 Celery, Cucumber and Zucchini Soup (p.20, Cal 325)

Lunch - 7.7 Veggies Stuffed Bell Peppers (p.31, Cal 213)

Snacks - 9.1 Soy Sauce Green Beans (p.44, Cal 46)

Dinner - 10.3 Chicken Bowl with Red Cabbage (p.52, Cal 261)

Nutrition Per Day:

Calories - 927 | Fat - 59g | Carbs - 102g | Protein - 48g | Sugar - 46g | Fiber - 23g | Potassium - 3136mg | Sodium - 787mg | Cholesterol - 134mg

Tuesday

Breakfast - 13.4 Chocolate Berry (p.70, Cal 319)

Snack - 5.7 Vegetable Barley & Turkey Soup (p.21, Cal 209)

Lunch - 7.8 Rosemary Endives (p.31, Cal 66)

Snacks - 9.15 Honey Sage Carrots (p.50, Cal 217)

Dinner - 10.4 Chicken Sandwich (p.52, Cal 265)

Nutrition Per Day:

Calories - 1076 | Fat - 45g | Carbs - 89g | Protein - 37.3g | Sugar - 29.3g | Fiber - 44g | Potassium - 4245mg | Sodium - 1453mg | Cholesterol - 298mg

Wednesday

Breakfast - 13.5 Tropical Turmeric (p.70, Cal 295)

Snacks - 5.8 Tomato Green Bean Soup (p.21, Cal 58)

Lunch - 7.9 Easy Chicken Veggie Burgers (p.32, Cal 118)

Snacks - 9.14 Italian Style Mushroom Mix (p.50, Cal 96)

Dinner - 10.5 Turkey and Zucchini Tortillas (p.53, Cal 260)

Nutrition Per Day:

Calories - 827 | Fat - 27g Carbs - 102g | Protein - 45g | Sugar - 61.9g | Fiber - 29.8g | Potassium - 2815mg | Sodium - 695mg | Cholesterol - 153mg

Thursday

Breakfast - 13.6 Carrot Juice Smoothie (p.70, Cal 241)

Snacks - 5.9 Mushroom Barley Soup (p.22, Cal 129)

Lunch - 7.10 Baked Sweet Potatoes with Cumin (p.32, Cal 264)

Snacks - 9.13 Parsley Red Potatoes (p.49, Cal 256)

Dinner - 10.6 Chicken with Eggplants (p.53, Cal 260)

Nutrition Per Day:

Calories - 1150 | Fat - 33g | Carbs - 181g | Protein - 53g | Sugar - 58g | Fiber - 42g | Potassium - 2138mg | Sodium - 1175mg | Cholesterol - 76mg

Friday

Breakfast - 13.7 Mixed Berries Smoothie (p.70, Cal 130)

Snacks - 14.1 Corn and Cayenne pepper Spread (p.74, Cal 70)

Lunch - 7.11 White Beans with Spinach and Pan-Roasted Tomatoes (p.33, Cal 293)

Snacks - 9.12 Parsley Fennel (p.49, Cal 47)

Dinner - 10.7 Garlic Turkey (p.54, Cal 170)

Nutrition Per Day:

Calories - 710 | Fat - 22g | Carbs - 94g | Protein - 48g | Sugar - 14g | Fiber - 30g | Potassium - 1525mg | Sodium - 631mg | Cholesterol - 61mg

Saturday

Breakfast - 13.8 Satisfying Berry and Almond Smoothie (p.71, Cal 138)

Snacks - 14.2 Black Bean Bars (p.74, Cal 90)

Lunch - 7.12 Black-Eyed Peas and Green Power Salad (p.33, Cal 320)

Snacks - 9.11 Carrot Sticks with Onion and Sour Cream (p.48, Cal 60)

Dinner - 10.8 Cheddar Turkey (p.54, Cal 301)

Nutrition Per Day:

Calories - 909 | Fat - 21.1g | Carbs - 97.2g | Protein - 51.6g | Sugar - 30.4g | Fiber - 48.6g | Potassium - 2076mg | Sodium - 1788mg | Cholesterol - 118mg

Sunday

Breakfast - 13.9 Refreshing Mango and Pear Smoothie (p.71, Cal 244)

Snacks - 14.3 Roasted Red Pepper and Chickpea Hummus (p.74, Cal 160)

Lunch - 7.13 Butternut-Squash Macaroni and Cheese (p.34, Cal 373)

Snacks - 9.10 Pomegranate & Ricotta Bruschetta (p.48, Cal 69)

Dinner - 10.9 Parsnip and Turkey Bites (p.55, Cal 190)

Nutrition Per Day:

Calories - 1036 | Fat - 23g | Carbs - 154g | Protein - 60.5g | Sugar - 74g | Fiber - 44g | Potassium - 2362mg | Sodium - 846mg | Cholesterol - 174mg

16.4 Week 4

Monday

Breakfast - 13.10 Blackberry and Apple Smoothie (p.71, Cal 130)

Snacks - 14.4 Lemon and Coriander Chickpea Dip (p.75, Cal 160)

Lunch - 7.14 Pasta with Peas & Tomatoes (p.34, Cal 266)

Snacks - 9.9 Fresh Fruit Kebabs (p.48, Cal 27)

Dinner - 10.10 Nutmeg Chicken with Tender Chickpeas (p.55, Cal 387)

Nutrition Per Day:

Calories - 970 | Fat - 42g | Carbs - 140g | Protein - 64g | Sugar - 57.4g | Fiber - 43g | Potassium - 1764mg | Sodium - 1677mg | Cholesterol - 56mg

Tuesday

Breakfast - 13.11 Raspberry Green Smoothie (p.71, Cal 269)

Snacks - 14.5 Red Pepper and Mozzarella Muffins (p.75, Cal 120)

Lunch - 7.15 Healthy Vegetable Fried Rice (p.35, Cal 210)

Snacks - 9.8 Chinese-Style Asparagus (p.47, Cal 260)

Dinner - 10.11 Green Chilli Turkey (p.56, Cal 180)

Nutrition Per Day:

Calories - 1039 | Fat - 35g | Carbs - 114g | Protein - 71g | Sugar - 34g | Fiber - 40g | Potassium - 2063mg | Sodium - 410mg | Cholesterol - 457mg

Wednesday

Breakfast - 13.12 Blueberry Smoothie (p.72, Cal 114)

Snacks - 14.6 Nuts and Seed Trail Mix (p.76, Cal 280)

Lunch - 7.16 Cast Iron Roots and Grain (p.35, Cal 312)

Snacks - 9.7 Mashed Cauliflower with Garlic (p.47, Cal 67)

Dinner - 10.12 Hot Chicken Mix (p.56, Cal 190)

Nutrition Per Day:

Calories - 963 | Fat - 41.5g | Carbs - 117g | Protein - 45.9g | Sugar - 45.4g | Fiber - 28g | Potassium - 2263mg | Sodium - 381mg | Cholesterol - 68mg

Thursday

Breakfast - 13.14 Chocolate and Peanut Butter Smoothie (p.72, Cal 336)

Snacks - 14.7 Baked Tortilla Chips with Chilli (p.76, Cal 90)

Lunch - 7.17 Easy Beet and Goat Cheese Risotto (p.36, Cal 413)

Snacks - 9.6 Spiced Broccoli Florets (p.46, Cal 119)

Dinner - 10.13 Mustard and Garlic Chicken (p.57, Cal 230)

Nutrition Per Day:

Calories - 1188 | Fat - 71g | Carbs - 89g | Protein - 65g | Sugar - 34g | Fiber - 23g | Potassium - 1914mg | Sodium - 766mg | Cholesterol - 192mg

Friday

Breakfast - 13.15 Ultimate Fruit Smoothie (p.72, Cal 150)

Snacks - 14.7 Baked Tortilla Chips with Chili (p.76, Cal 90)

Lunch - 7.18 Mushroom and Eggplant Casserole (p.36, Cal 340)

Snacks - 9.5 Chive & Garlic Mash (p.46, Cal 292)

Dinner - 10.14 Boneless Chicken Curry (p.57, Cal 220)

Nutrition Per Day:

Calories - 1092 | Fat - 35g | Carbs - 98g | Protein - 69g | Sugar - 29g | Fiber - 21g | Potassium - 2734mg | Sodium - 854mg | Cholesterol - 132mg

Saturday

Breakfast - 13.16 Oat Cocoa Smoothie (p.73, Cal 180)

Snacks - 14.9 Hearty Walnut Butter Bites (p.77, Cal 120)

Lunch - 7.19 Spinach Souffles (p.37, Cal 152)

Snacks - 9.4 Peach And Carrots (p.45, Cal 139)

Dinner - 10.15 Chicken with Tomatoes (p.58, Cal 180)

Nutrition Per Day:

Calories - 771 | Fat - 41g | Carbs - 87g | Protein - 51g | Sugar - 23g | Fiber - 15g | Potassium - 1544mg | Sodium - 511mg | Cholesterol - 169mg

Sunday

Breakfast - 13.17 Tropical Green Breakfast Smoothie (p.73, Cal 180)

Snacks - 14.10 Spiced Walnuts (p.82, Cal 260)

Lunch - 7.20 Huevos Rancheros (p.37, Cal 152)

Snacks - 9.3 Cumin Brussels Sprouts (p.45, Cal 56)

Dinner - 10.16 Basil Turkey (p.58, Cal 150)

Nutrition Per Day:

Calories - 798 | Fat - 41g | Carbs - 65g | Protein - 53g | Sugar - 25g | Fiber - 15g | Potassium - 1677mg | Sodium - 340mg | Cholesterol - 166mg

16.5 Week 5

Monday

Breakfast - 13.18 Green Apple Smoothie (p.72, Cal 120)

Snacks - 14.11 Radish Chips (p.78, Cal 90)

Lunch - 7.21 Eggplant Special (p.38, Cal 203)

Snacks - 9.2 Sour Cream Green Beans (p.44, Cal 360)

Dinner - 11.1 Pork with Cherry Tomatoes (p.59, Cal 210)

Nutrition Per Day:

Calories - 983 | Fat - 34g | Carbs - 119g | Protein - 58g | Sugar - 35g | Fiber - 17g | Potassium - 2706mg | Sodium - 624mg | Cholesterol - 230mg

Tuesday

Breakfast - 3.1 Millet Cream (p.11, Cal 989)

Snacks - 14.12 Aromatic Avocado Fries (p.78, Cal 90)

Lunch - 7.22 Zucchini Black Bean Tacos (p.38, Cal 245)

Snacks - 9.1 Soy Sauce Green Beans (p.44, Cal 46)

Dinner - 11.2 Thyme Pork Skillet (p.59, Cal 274)

Nutrition Per Day:

Calories - 1644 | Fat - 34g | Carbs - 68g | Protein - 51g | Sugar - 0.2034g | Fiber - 17g | Potassium - 2096mg | Sodium - 466mg | Cholesterol - 171mg

Wednesday

Breakfast - 3.2 The Amazing Feta Hash (p.11, Cal 303)
Snacks - 14.13 Carrot Chips (p.78, Cal 90)
Lunch - 7.23 Polenta Squares with Cheese & Pine Nuts (p.39, Cal 130)
Snacks - 9.15 Honey Sage Carrots (p.50, Cal 217)
Dinner - 11.3 Meat and Zucchini Mix (p.60, Cal 359)
Nutrition Per Day:
Calories - 1099 | Fat - 24g | Carbs - 70g | Protein - 77g | Sugar - 26g | Fiber - 21g | Potassium - 2813mg | Sodium - 887mg | Cholesterol - 327mg

Thursday

Breakfast - 3.3 Sausage Casserole (p.12, Cal 74)
Snacks - 14.14 Minty Tapenade (p.78, Cal 180)
Lunch - 8.1 Vegetarian Black Bean Pasta (p.40, Cal 255)
Snacks - 9.14 Italians Style Mushroom Mix (p.50, Cal 96)
Dinner - 11.4 Garlic Pork (p.60, Cal 344)
Nutrition Per Day:
Calories - 949 | Fat - 49g | Carbs - 82g | Protein - 50g | Sugar - 19g | Fiber - 29g | Potassium - 1648mg | Sodium - 445mg | Cholesterol - 180mg

Friday

Breakfast - 3.4 Apples and Raisins Bowls (p.12, Cal 266)
Snacks - 14.15 Nutritious Snack Bowls (p.79, Cal 180)
Lunch - 8.2 Lentil Medley (p.40, Cal 225)
Snacks - 9.13 Parsley Red Potatoes (p.49, Cal 256)
Dinner - 11.5 Beef with Cauliflower Rice (p.61, Cal 449)
Nutrition Per Day:
Calories - 1376 | Fat - 47g | Carbs - 147g | Protein - 57g | Sugar - 56g | Fiber - 60g | Potassium - 4251mg | Sodium - 1654mg | Cholesterol - 365mg

Saturday

Breakfast - 3.5 Dill Omelet (p.12, Cal 71)
Snacks - 14.16 Potato Chips (p.79, Cal 180)
Lunch - 8.3 Zucchini with Corn (p.41, Cal 202)
Snacks - 9.12 Parsley Fennel (p.49, Cal 47)
Dinner - 11.6 Cilantro Beef Meatballs (p.61, Cal 502)
Nutrition Per Day:
Calories - 1002 | Fat - 40g | Carbs - 90g | Protein - 86g | Sugar - 10g | Fiber - 33g | Potassium - 3341mg | Sodium - 612mg | Cholesterol - 411mg

Sunday

Breakfast - 3.6 Cheese Hash Browns (p.12, Cal 212)
Snacks - 14.17 Hot Walnuts (p.79, Cal 180)
Lunch - 8.4 Couscous with Beans & Vegetables (p.41, Cal 330)
Snacks - 9.11 Carrot Sticks with Onion & Sour Cream (p.48, Cal 60)
Dinner - 11.7 Spiced Meat with Endives (p.62, Cal 288)
Nutrition Per Day:
Calories - 1070 | Fat - 46.6g | Carbs - 103.2g | Protein - 61.2g | Sugar - 47mg | Fiber - 58.6g | Potassium - 5571mg | Sodium - 769mg | Cholesterol - 211mg

16.6 Week 6

Monday

Breakfast - 3.7 Tomato and Spinach Eggs (p.13, Cal 202)
Snacks - 14.18 Cranberry Crackers (p.79, Cal)
Lunch - 8.5 Roasted Kabocha with Wild Rice (p.42, Cal 250)
Snacks - 9.10 Pomegranate & Ricotta Bruschetta (p.48, Cal 69)
Dinner - 6.1 Cilantro Halibut (p.23, Cal 365)
Nutrition Per Day:
Calories - 1066 | Fat - 48.2g | Carbs - 74g | Protein - 89g | Sugar - 39g | Fiber - 31g | Potassium - 2963mg | Sodium - 657mg | Cholesterol - 523mg

Tuesday

Breakfast - 3.8 Scallions and Sesame Seeds Omelet (p.13, Cal 101)
Snacks - 4.1 Shrimp and Veggie Salad (p.20, Cal 390)
Lunch - 8.6 Acorn Squash & Coconut Creamed Greens Casserole (p.42, Cal 248)
Snacks - 9.9 Fresh Fruit Kebabs (p.48, Cal 27)
Dinner - 6.2 Shallot and Salmon Mix (p.23, Cal 369)
Nutrition Per Day:
Calories - 1135 | Fat - 73g | Carbs - 82g | Protein - 91g | Sugar - 38g | Fiber - 23g | Potassium - 2596mg | Sodium - 907mg | Cholesterol - 482mg

Wednesday

Breakfast - 3.9 Omelet with Peppers (p.13, Cal 102)
Snacks - 4.2 Salmon and Spinach (p.20, Cal 155)
Lunch - 8.8 Curried Cauliflower with Chickpeas (p.43, Cal 224)
Snacks - 9.8 Chinese-Style Asparagus (p.47, Cal 260)
Dinner - 6.3 Lime and Shrimp Skewers (p.23, Cal 141)
Nutrition Per Day:
Calories - 882 | Fat - 21g | Carbs - 80g | Protein - 87g | Sugar - 13g | Fiber - 32.5g | Potassium - 3474mg | Sodium - 1031mg | Cholesterol - 603mg

Thursday

Breakfast - 3.10 Artichoke Eggs (p.13, Cal 176)
Snacks - 4.3 Corn Salad (p.21, Cal 159)
Lunch - 7.1 Roasted Brussels Sprouts (p.28, Cal 70)
Snacks - 9.7 Mashed Cauliflower with Garlic (p.47, Cal 67)
Dinner - 6.4 Tuna and Pineapple Kabob (p.24, Cal 135)
Nutrition Per Day:
Calories - 607 | Fat - 20g | Carbs - 71.6g | Protein - 42.4g | Sugar - 30g | Fiber - 46g | Potassium - 1670mg | Sodium - 923mg | Cholesterol - 291mg

Friday

Breakfast - 3.11 Bean Casserole (p.14, Cal 143)
Snacks - 4.4 Watercress Salad (p. , Cal 264)
Lunch - 7.2 Chunky Black-Bean Dip (p.28, Cal 70)
Snacks - 9.6 Spiced Broccoli Florets (p.46, Cal 119)
Dinner - 6.56.5 Coconut Cod (p.24, Cal 191)
Nutrition Per Day:
Calories - 787 | Fat - 36g | Carbs - 43g | Protein - 78g | Sugar - 7g | Fiber - 33.8g | Potassium - 2840mg | Sodium - 1065mg | Cholesterol - 469mg

Saturday

Breakfast - 3.12 Strawberry Sandwich (p.14, Cal 84)
Snacks - 4.5 Tuna Salad (p. , Cal 173)
Lunch - 7.3 Greek Flat bread with Spinach, Tomatoes & Feta (p.29, Cal 410)
Snacks - 9.5 Chive & Garlic Mash (p.46, Cal 292)
Dinner - 6.4 Tuna and Pineapple Kabob (p.24, Cal 135)
Nutrition Per Day:
Calories - 1094 | Fat - 40g | Carbs - 148g | Protein - 48.4g | Sugar - 26g | Fiber - 21g | Potassium - 2642mg | Sodium - 1383mg | Cholesterol - 48mg

Sunday

Breakfast - 13.1 Blueberry-Vanilla Yogurt Smoothie (p.69, Cal 186)
Snacks - 4.4 Watercress Salad (p.21, Cal 264)
Lunch - 7.4 Black-Bean and Vegetable Burrito (p.29, Cal 311)
Snacks - 9.4 Peach And Carrots (p.45, Cal 139)
Dinner - 6.5 Coconut Cod (p.24, Cal 191)
Nutrition Per Day:
Calories - 1091 | Fat - 41g | Carbs - 136g | Protein - 88g | Sugar - 31g | Fiber - 34g | Potassium - 2766mg | Sodium - 932mg | Cholesterol - 332mg

16.7 Week 7

Monday

Breakfast - 13.2 Peaches And Greens Smoothie (p.69, Cal 105)
Snacks - 4.7 Orange Celery Salad (p.22, Cal 65)
Lunch - 7.5 Red Beans and Rice (p.30, Cal 232)
Snacks - 9.3 Cumin Brussels Sprouts (p.45, Cal 56)
Dinner - 6.6 Ginger Sea Bass (p.24, Cal 191)
Nutrition Per Day:
Calories - 649 | Fat - 19g | Carbs - 82g | Protein - 49g | Sugar - 22g | Fiber - 36g | Potassium - 1828mg | Sodium - 525mg | Cholesterol - 95mg

Tuesday

Breakfast - 13.3 Banana Breakfast Smoothie (p.69, Cal 82)
Snacks - 4.8 Lettuce & Cucumber Salad (p.22, Cal 88)
Lunch - 7.6 Veggie Pita Rolls (p.30, Cal 334)
Snacks - 9.2 Sour Cream Green Beans (p.44, Cal 360)
Dinner - 6.6 Ginger Sea Bass (p.24, Cal 191)
Nutrition Per Day:
Calories - 1055 | Fat - 37g | Carbs - 174g | Protein - 61g | Sugar - 50g | Fiber - 26g | Potassium - 2845mg | Sodium - 858mg | Cholesterol - 147mg

Wednesday

Breakfast - 13.4 Chocolate Berry Smoothie (p.70, Cal 319)
Snacks - 4.8 Lettuce & Cucumber Salad (p.22, Cal 88)
Lunch - 7.7 Veggies Stuffed Bell Peppers (p.31, Cal 213)
Snacks - 9.1 Soy Sauce Green Beans (p.44, Cal 46)
Dinner - 6.7 Baked Cod (p.25, Cal 150)
Nutrition Per Day:
Calories - 816 | Fat - 48g | Carbs - 62g | Protein - 42g | Sugar - 17g | Fiber - 28g | Potassium - 1765mg | Sodium - 390mg | Cholesterol - 95mg

Thursday

Breakfast - 13.5 Tropical Turmeric Smoothie (p.70, Cal 295)
Snacks - 4.9 Seafood Arugula Salad (p.22, Cal 155)
Lunch - 7.8 Rosemary Endives (p.31, Cal 66)
Snacks - 9.15 Honey sage carrots (p.50, Cal 217)
Dinner - 6.8 Five-Spices Sole (p.25, Cal 180)
Nutrition Per Day:
Calories - 913 | Fat - 40g | Carbs - 54g | Protein - 49g | Sugar - 35g | Fiber - 17g | Potassium - 1872mg | Sodium - 989mg | Cholesterol - 391mg

Friday

Breakfast - 13.6 Carrot Juice Smoothie (p.70, Cal 241)

Snacks - 5.1 Lemon & Garlic Soup (p.23, Cal 101)

Lunch - 7.9 Easy Chickpea Veggie Burgers (p.32, Cal 118)

Snacks - 9.14 Italians Style Mushroom Mix (p.50, Cal 96)

Dinner - 6.9 Parsley Shrimp (p.25, Cal 120)

Nutrition Per Day:

Calories - 676 | Fat - 23g | Carbs - 78g | Protein - 38g | Sugar - 54.9mg | Fiber - 46.8g | Potassium - 4042mg | Sodium - 803mg | Cholesterol - 233mg

Saturday

Breakfast - 13.7 Mixed Berries Smoothie (p.70, Cal 130)

Snacks - 5.2 Healthy Cucumber Soup (p.23, Cal 371)

Lunch - 7.10 Baked Sweet Potatoes with Cumin (p.32, Cal 264)

Snacks - 9.13 Parsley Red Potatoes (p.49, Cal 256)

Dinner - 6.10 Tender Salmon with Chives (p.26, Cal 250)

Nutrition Per Day:

Calories - 1271 | Fat - 62g | Carbs - 124g | Protein - 56g | Sugar - 30mg | Fiber - 42g | Potassium - 1360mg | Sodium - 1328mg | Cholesterol - 66mg

Sunday

Breakfast - 13.8 Satisfying Berry and Almond Smoothie (p.71, Cal 138)

Snacks - 5.3 Amazing Pumpkin Soup (p.24, Cal 61)

Lunch - 7.11 White Beans with Spinach and Pan-Roasted Tomatoes (p.33, Cal 293)

Snacks - 9.12 Parsley Fennel (p.49, Cal 47)

Dinner - 6.11 Fennel and Salmon (p.26, Cal 250)

Nutrition Per Day:

Calories - 789 | Fat - 33g | Carbs - 91g | Protein - 48g | Sugar - 16.4mg | Fiber - 31g | Potassium - 1922mg | Sodium - 731mg | Cholesterol - 70mg

16.8 Week 8

Monday

Breakfast - 13.9 Refreshing Mango and Pear Smoothie (p.71, Cal 244)

Snacks - 5.4 Coconut Avocado Soup (p.24, Cal 250)

Lunch - 7.12 Black-Eyed Peas and greens Power Salad (p.33, Cal 320)

Snacks - 9.11 Carrot Sticks with Onion and Sour Cream (p.48, Cal 60)

Dinner - 6.12 Cod and Asparagus (p.27, Cal 190)

Nutrition Per Day:
Calories - 1064 | Fat - 50.1g | Carbs - 113.2g | Protein - 64.1g | Sugar - 34mg | Fiber - 57.6g | Potassium - 3147mg | Sodium - 569mg | Cholesterol - 101mg

Tuesday

Breakfast - 13.10 Blackberry and Apple Smoothie (p.71, Cal 130)

Snacks – 5.5 Pumpkin and Garlic Soup (p.90, Cal 90)

Lunch - 7.13 Butternut-Squash Macaroni and Cheese (p.34, Cal 373)

Snacks - 9.10 Pomegranate & Ricotta Bruschetta (p.48, Cal 69)

Dinner - 10.1 Turkey with Spring Onions (p.51, Cal 179)

Nutrition Per Day:
Calories - 841 | Fat - 25g | Carbs - 113g | Protein - 49g | Sugar - 65mg | Fiber - 39g | Potassium - 1393mg | Sodium - 621mg | Cholesterol - 172mg

Wednesday

Breakfast - 13.11 Raspberry Green Smoothie (p.71, Cal 269)

Snacks - 14.1 Corn and Cayenne Pepper Spread (p.74, Cal 70)

Lunch - 7.14 Pasta with Peas & Tomatoes (p.34, Cal 266)

Snacks - 9.9 Fresh Fruit Kebabs (p.48, Cal 27)

Dinner - 10.210.2 Chicken with Tomatoes and Celery Stalk (p.51, Cal 265)

Nutrition Per Day:
Calories - 897 | Fat - 43.2g | Carbs - 112.5g | Protein - 71g | Sugar - 59mg | Fiber - 41g | Potassium - 1950mg | Sodium - 506mg | Cholesterol - 106mg

Thursday

Breakfast - 13.12 Blueberry Smoothie (p.72, Cal 114)

Snacks - 14.2 Black Bean Bars (p.74, Cal 90)

Lunch - Error! Reference source not found. Healthy Vegetable Fried Rice (p.35, Cal 210)

Snacks - 9.8 Chinese-Style Asparagus (p.47, Cal 260)

Dinner - 10.3 Chicken Bowl with Red Cabbage (p.52, Cal 261)

Nutrition Per Day -
Calories - 935 | Fat - 18.5g | Carbs - 118g | Protein - 70g | Sugar - 40.4mg | Fiber - 33g | Potassium - 2431mg | Sodium - 311mg | Cholesterol - 445mg

Friday

Breakfast - 13.13 Avocado Smoothie (p.72, Cal 243)

Snacks - 14.3 Roasted Red Pepper and Chickpea Hummus (p.74, Cal 160)

Lunch - 7.16 Cast Iron Roots and Grain (p.35, Cal 312)

Snacks - 9.7 Mashed Cauliflower with Garlic (p.47, Cal 67)

Dinner - 10.4 Chicken Sandwich (p.52, Cal 265)

Nutrition Per Day:
Calories - 1047 | Fat - 45g | Carbs - 133g | Protein - 45.9g | Sugar - 27mg | Fiber - 37g | Potassium - 2153mg | Sodium - 754mg | Cholesterol - 47mg

Saturday

Breakfast - 13.14 Chocolate and Peanut Butter Smoothie (p.72, Cal 336)

Snacks - 14.4 Lemon and Coriander Chickpea Dip (p.75, Cal 160)

Lunch - 7.17 Easy Beet and Goat Cheese Risotto (p.36, Cal 413)

Snacks - 9.6 Spiced Broccoli Florets (p.46, Cal 119)

Dinner - 10.5 Turkey and Zucchini Tortillas (p.53, Cal 260)

Nutrition Per Day:
Calories - 1288 | Fat - 71g | Carbs - 122g | Protein - 61g | Sugar - 32mg | Fiber - 27g | Potassium - 2064mg | Sodium - 816mg | Cholesterol - 161mg

Sunday

Breakfast - 13.15 Ultimate Fruit Smoothie (p.72, Cal 150)
Snacks - 14.5 Red Pepper and Mozzarella Muffins (p.75, Cal 120)
Lunch - 7.17 Easy Beet and Goat Cheese Risotto (p.36, Cal 413)
Snacks - 9.5 Chive & Garlic Mash (p.46, Cal 292)
Dinner - 10.6 Chicken with Eggplants (p.53, Cal 260)
Nutrition Per Day:
Calories - 1234.5 | Fat - 65g | Carbs - 126g | Protein - 59g | Sugar - 45.9mg | Fiber - 22g | Potassium - 2763mg | Sodium - 882mg | Cholesterol - 173mg

16.9 Week 9

Monday

Breakfast - 13.16 Oat Cocoa Smoothie (p.73, Cal 180)
Snacks - 14.6 Nuts And Seed Trail Mix (p.76, Cal 280)
Lunch - 7.18 Mushroom and Eggplant Casserole (p.36, Cal 340)
Snacks - 9.4 Peach And Carrots (p.45, Cal 139)
Dinner - 10.7 Garlic Turkey (p.54, Cal 170)
Nutrition Per Day:
Calories - 1109 | Fat - 56g | Carbs - 115g | Protein - 62g | Sugar - 39mg | Fiber - 24g | Potassium - 1909mg | Sodium - 655mg | Cholesterol - 120mg

Tuesday

Breakfast - 13.5 Tropical Turmeric Smoothie (p.73, Cal 180)
Snacks - 14.7 Baked Tortilla Chips with Chili (p.76, Cal 90)
Lunch - 7.18 Mushroom and Eggplant Casserole (p.36, Cal 340)
Snacks - 9.3 Cumin Brussels Sprouts (p.45, Cal 56)
Dinner - 10.8 Cheddar Turkey (p.54, Cal 301)
Nutrition Per Day:
Calories - 967 | Fat - 20g | Carbs - 85g | Protein - 64g | Sugar - 35.4mg | Fiber - 23g | Potassium - 2099mg | Sodium - 1662mg | Cholesterol - 140mg

Wednesday

Breakfast - 13.18 Green Apple Smoothie (p.73, Cal 120)
Snacks - 14.8 Baked Kale Chips (p.77, Cal 30)
Lunch - 7.19 Spinach Soufflés (p.37, Cal 152)
Snacks - 9.2 Sour Cream Green Beans (p.44, Cal 360)
Dinner - 10.9 Parsnip and Turkey Bites (p.55, Cal 190)
Nutrition Per Day:
Calories - 852 | Fat - 22.2g | Carbs - 115g | Protein - 56g | Sugar - 31.5mg | Fiber - 12g | Potassium - 2566mg | Sodium - 693mg | Cholesterol - 181mg

Thursday

Breakfast - 3.1 Millet Cream (p.16, Cal 989)
Snacks - 14.9 Hearty Walnut Butter Bites (p.77, Cal 120)
Lunch - 7.20 Huevos Rancheros (p.37, Cal 152)
Snacks - 9.1 Soy Sauce green Beans (p.44, Cal 46)
Dinner - 10.10 Nutmeg Chicken with Tender Chickpeas (p.55, Cal 387)
Nutrition Per Day:
Calories - 1694 | Fat - 34.5g | Carbs - 95g | Protein - 54g | Sugar - 203mg | Fiber - 17g | Potassium - 2215mg | Sodium - 1601mg | Cholesterol - 223mg

Friday

Breakfast - 3.2 The Amazing Feta Hash (p.16, Cal 303)
Snacks - 14.10 Spiced Walnuts (p.77, Cal 260)
Lunch - 7.21 Eggplant Special (p.38, Cal 203)
Snacks - 9.15 Honey sage carrots (p.50, Cal 217)
Dinner - 10.11 Green Chilli Turkey (p.56, Cal 180)
Nutrition Per Day:
Calories - 1163 | Fat   49g | Carbs - 65g | Protein - 55g | Sugar - 22.7mg | Fiber - 23g| Potassium - 2178mg | Sodium - 821mg | Cholesterol - 310mg

Saturday

Breakfast - 3.3 Sausage Casserole (p.17, Cal 74)
Snacks - 14.11 Radish Chips (p.78, Cal 90)
Lunch - 7.22 Zucchini Black Bean Tacos (p.38, Cal 245)
Snacks - 9.14 Italians Style Mushroom Mix (p.50, Cal 96)
Dinner - 10.12 Hot Chicken Mix (p.56, Cal 190)
Nutrition Per Day:
Calories - 695 | Fat - 32g | Carbs - 43g | Protein - 42g | Sugar - 5.7mg | Fiber - 19.8g | Potassium - 1707mg | Sodium - 512mg | Cholesterol - 161mg

Sunday

Breakfast - 3.4 Apples and Raisins Bowls (p.17, Cal 266)
Snacks - 14.12 Aromatic Avocado Fries (p.78, Cal 90)
Lunch - 7.23 Polenta Squares with Cheese & Pine Nuts (p.39, Cal 130)
Snacks - 9.13 Parsley Red Potatoes (p.49, Cal 256)
Dinner - 10.13 Mustard and garlic Chicken (p.57, Cal 230)
Nutrition Per Day:
Calories - 972 | Fat - 33.2g | Carbs - 84g | Protein - 44.5g | Sugar - 13.3mg | Fiber - 19g| Potassium - 1384mg | Sodium - 1198mg | Cholesterol - 402mg

16.10 Week 10

Monday

Breakfast - 3.5 Dill Omelet (p.17, Cal 71)
Snacks - 14.13 Carrot Chips (p.78, Cal 90)
Lunch - 8.1 Vegetarian Black Bean Pasta (p.40, Cal 255)
Snacks - 9.12 Parsley Fennel (p.49, Cal 47)
Dinner - 10.1410.14 Boneless Chicken Curry (p.57, Cal 220)
Nutrition Per Day:
Calories - 683 | Fat - 17g | Carbs - 71g | Protein - 51g | Sugar - 8mg | Fiber - 22.3g | Potassium - 1748mg | Sodium - 411mg | Cholesterol - 232mg

Tuesday

Breakfast - 3.6 Cheese Hash Browns (p.17, Cal 212)
Snacks - 14.14 Minty Tapenade (p.78, Cal 180)
Lunch - 8.2 Lentil Medley (p.40, Cal 225)
Snacks - 9.11 Carrot Sticks with Onion & Sour Cream (p.48, Cal 60)
Dinner - 10.15 Chicken with Tomatoes (p.58, Cal 180)
Nutrition Per Day:
Calories - 857 | Fat - 41.1g | Carbs - 84.4g | Protein - 41.2g | Sugar - 57mg | Fiber - 61g| Potassium - 4722mg | Sodium - 829mg | Cholesterol - 179mg

Wednesday

Breakfast - 3.7 Tomato and Spinach Eggs (p.18, Cal 202)
Snacks - 14.14 Minty Tapenade (p.78, Cal 180)
Lunch - 8.3 Zucchini with Corn (p.45, Cal 202)
Snacks - 9.10 Pomegranate & Ricotta Bruschetta (p.48, Cal 69)
Dinner - 10.16 Basil Turkey (p.58, Cal 150)
Nutrition Per Day:
Calories - 803 | Fat - 34g | Carbs - 81g | Protein - 55g | Sugar - 35.3mg | Fiber - 48g| Potassium - 2290mg | Sodium - 595mg | Cholesterol - 492mg

Thursday

Breakfast - 3.8 Scallions and Sesame Seeds Omelet (p.18, Cal 101)
Calories - 101
Snacks - 14.15 Nutritious Snack Bowls (p.79, Cal 180)
Lunch - 8.4 Couscous with Beans & Vegetables (p.45, Cal 330)
Snacks - 9.9 Fresh Fruit Kebabs (p.48, Cal 27)
Dinner - 11.1 Pork with Cherry Tomatoes (p.59, Cal 210)
Nutrition Per Day:
Calories - 848 | Fat - 38.5g Carbs - 112g | Protein - 64g | Sugar - 73mg | Fiber - 57g | Potassium - 5110mg | Sodium - 428mg | Cholesterol - 256mg

Friday

Breakfast - 3.9 Omelet with Peppers (p.18, Cal 102)
Snacks - 14.16 Potato Chips (p.79, Cal 180)
Lunch - 8.5 Roasted Kabocha with Wild Rice (p.42, Cal 250)
Snacks - 9.8 Chinese-Style Asparagus (p.47, Cal 260)
Dinner - 11.2 Thyme Pork Skillet (p.59, Cal 274)
Nutrition Per Day:
Calories - 1066 | Fat - 47g | Carbs - 80g | Protein - 74g | Sugar - 11g | Fiber - 15g | Potassium - 2455mg | Sodium - 446mg | Cholesterol - 257mg

Saturday

Breakfast - 3.10 Artichoke Eggs (p.18, Cal 176)
Snacks - 14.17 Hot Walnuts (p.79, Cal 180)
Lunch - 8.6 Acorn Squash & Coconut Creamed Greens Casserole (p.42, Cal 248)
Snacks - 9.7 Mashed Cauliflower with garlic (p.47, Cal 67)
Dinner - 11.3 Meat and Zucchini Mix (p.60, Cal 359)
Nutrition Per Day:
Calories - 1030 | Fat - 60.4g | Carbs - 42.6g | Protein - 86g | Sugar - 9g | Fiber - 17g | Potassium - 2758mg | Sodium - 631mg | Cholesterol - 385mg

Sunday

Breakfast - 3.11 Bean Casserole (p.19, Cal 143)
Snacks - 14.18 Cranberry Crackers (p.79, Cal 180)
Lunch - 8.7 Warm Spiced Cabbage Bake (p.43, Cal 131)
Snacks - 9.6 Spiced Broccoli Florets (p.46, Cal 119)
Dinner - 11.4 Garlic Pork (p.60, Cal 344)
Nutrition Per Day:
Calories - 917 | Fat - 46g | Carbs - 65g | Protein - 69g | Sugar - 26g | Fiber - 43g | Potassium - 3340mg | Sodium - 663mg | Cholesterol - 220mg

17 CONCLUSION

Dash diet is an excellent choice for individuals who aspire to shed some weight and improve their wellness or health. It's also a diet plan you can follow without thinking of its side effects. If you're overweight or obese, then this diet will assist you in losing weight effectively, naturally, and simply because it focuses on whole foods that are rich in nutrients, unlike other diets, which include processed foods with artificial chemicals. The Dash diet program is an excellent approach to improving your overall health and quality of life through simple eating habits.

18 BONUS

Scanning the following QR code will take you to a web page where you can access 13 fantastic bonuses after leaving your email: 6 video courses and video recipes, 4 mobile apps, a printable weight log, a printable exercise log and an additional eating plan.

Link: https://BookHip.com/CFTVPRA

19 ANALYTICAL INDEX

20 ANNEX – A

STORAGE AND REHEATING

LEFTOVER FOOD	REFRIGERATION TIME	FREEZING TIME	SPECIAL INSTRUCTIONS
PASTA, RICE AND GRAINS	3-5 days	3 months	Store in air-tight containers to avoid moisture build-up; may require reheating with a splash of water.
VEGATBLES	3-4 days	1-2 months	Blanch before freezing to preserve
FRUITS	5-7 days (if cut)	2-6 months	Can become soft; store without cutting for best quality.
SALADS	3-5 days	Not Recommended	Don't freeze due to wilting and high moisture content.
SEAFOOD	1-2 days	3-6 months	Pack tightly; risk of freezer burn
MEAT	3-4 days	2-6 months	Avoid freezer burn by sealing tightly; flavor may diminish over extended time.
DAIRY ITEMS	1-2 days	1-2 months	Can experience separation or curdling; best used in cooked dishes after freezing.
SMOOTHIES	1-2 days	4-6 months	Store fruits and other ingredients in zip-lock bags to avoid moisture and items getting rotten
BAKED ITEMS	3-7 days	2-3 months	Allow to cool completely before freezing; frosting or fillings may change in texture.
SOUPS AND STEWS	3-4 days	4-6 months	Cool before freezing; might require mixing after thawing due to possible separation.

*NOTE: Best tip to store food items is to make divide your meals into smaller portion sizes that can be consumed at a single time. Place each portion in an airtight zip-lock bags. This tip might help support better freezing to avoid repeated reheating and save the nutritional content of foods.

21 ANNEX – B WASHING AND HANDLING

Importance of Proper Cleaning

Before delving into the intricacies of plant-based cooking, it's crucial to understand the importance of thoroughly washing fruits and vegetables. Doing so removes dirt, bacteria, and any pesticide residues, ensuring that your dishes are not only delicious but also safe to eat.

Step-by-Step Guide to Washing Produce

1. **Hand Hygiene:** First and foremost, before and after you prepare any fruits or vegetables, wash your hands thoroughly for at least 15-20 seconds using warm water and hand soap. This crucial step minimizes the transfer of bacteria to your food.

2. **Prepare Vinegar and Salt Solution:** Combine 1 1/3 cup of vinegar and 1 tablespoon of salt in a large bowl. Stir the mixture until both the vinegar and salt have completely dissolved. The vinegar serves as a natural disinfectant, while the salt aids in drawing out hidden microbes.

3. **Initial Rinse:** Fruits and vegetables should be initially rinsed under running water. It's essential to gently rub the surface to loosen dirt and any lingering pesticides. Avoid using soap or chemical cleansers as these can leave residues that are harmful if ingested.

4. **Soaking:** Different types of produce require different soaking times. For thin-skinned fruits and vegetables like berries and leafy greens, a 5-minute soak in the vinegar and salt solution is sufficient. Firm-skinned produce like apples and squash should be left in the solution for about 10 minutes. This step is critical for thorough disinfection.

5. **Scrubbing:** For hard and textured fruits or vegetables like melons, carrots, sweet potatoes, and cucumbers, utilize a clean vegetable brush to scrub their skins gently. This removes trapped dirt and microbes that a simple rinse may not eliminate.

6. **Rinsing Post-Soak:** After soaking and scrubbing, rinse the produce under running plain water to remove any lingering vinegar or salt. Make sure to rinse thoroughly to ensure that no residues are left behind.

7. **Drying:** Use a clean kitchen cloth or paper towel to dry the fruits and vegetables. This step is more than just for convenience; it further minimizes the chance of bacterial growth.

8. **Inspect and Cut:** Finally, inspect your produce for any damaged or bruised areas. Cut these away as they can harbor bacteria and negatively affect the quality and safety of your food. Designate separate cutting boards for fruits/vegetables and raw meats. Always wash boards with hot soapy water after use.

9. **Meat:** Wash hands, meat, and utensils with soap and hot water to prevent cross-contamination, then pat meat dry before seasoning or cooking. Follow proper cooking temperatures and times to ensure meat is safely prepared and cooked to the recommended internal temperature.

Extra Tips

- Leafy Greens: For leafy greens like kale and spinach, a salad spinner can be incredibly useful to remove excess water post-washing.
- Berry Care: Berries are delicate. Rinse them only before you're about to use them to prevent spoilage.
- Storing: Some fruits and vegetables like tomatoes and avocados should be stored at room temperature until they ripen; then, they can be refrigerated.

Remember, clean produce contributes to safe and delicious meals!

22 MEASUREMENT

Volume Equivalents (Dry)	
US STANDARD	METRIC
1/8 teaspoon	0.5 ml
1/4 teaspoon	1 ml
1/2 teaspoon	2 ml
3/4 teaspoon	4 ml
1 teaspoon	5 ml
1 tablespoon	15 ml
1/4 cup	59 ml
1/2 cup	118 ml
3/4 cup	177 ml
1 cup	235 ml
2 cups	475 ml
3 cups	700 ml
4 cups	1 L

Volume Equivalents (Liquid)		
US STANDARD	US STANDARD (OUNCES)	METRIC (APPROX.)
2 tablespoons	1 fl. oz.	30 ml
1/4 cup	2 fl. oz.	60 ml
1/2 cup	4 fl. oz.	120 ml
1 cup	8 fl. oz.	240 ml
1 1/2 cup	12 fl. oz.	355 ml
2 cups or 1 pint	16 fl. oz.	475 ml
4 cups or 1 quart	32 fl. oz.	1 L
1 gallon	128 fl. oz.	4 L

Weight Equivalents	
US STANDARD	METRIC (APPROXIMATE)
1 ounce	28 g
2 ounces	57 g
5 ounces	142 g
10 ounces	284 g
15 ounces	425 g
16 ounces (1 pound)	455 g
1.5 pounds	680 g
2 pounds	907 g

Temperature Equivalents	
FAHR.(F)	METRIC
225 °F	107 °C
250 °F	120 °C
275 °F	135 °C
300 °F	150 °C
325 °F	160 °C
350 °F	180 °C
375 °F	190 °C
400 °F	205 °C
425 °F	220 °C
450 °F	235 °C
475 °F	245 °C

Printed in Great Britain
by Amazon

38427188R00059